Building a Road to Nuclear Disarmament

This book while comprehending the contemporary global security environment, offers a new roadmap for nuclear disarmament by creating a balance between deterrence supporters and disarmament advocators.

The author identifies the divide between competing approaches such as traditional security-centric aspects and humanity-centred disarmament perspectives, tackling the complex question of how to balance some states' compulsions for effective nuclear deterrence with other states' long-term desire for a nuclear-free world. The book explores how new technologies such as cyber and Artificial Intelligence advances are available to more countries than nuclear technology, and could level the playing field for weaker nuclear weapon states. It also looks into the issues which continue to be obstacles in the way of convincing the nuclear weapon states on nuclear disarmament. The author argues that the gap between states' security needs and disarmament aspirations can be bridged by building a new roadmap and creating new security environment.

This volume will be of great interest to students and scholars, researchers, policymakers, NGOs and members of the diplomatic community, in the fields of security studies, strategic studies and nuclear policy.

Rizwana Abbasi is an Associate Professor and Head of the Department of International Relations and Peace and Conflict Studies at the National University of Modern Languages in Islamabad, Pakistan. She has taught at many universities in Pakistan, the United Kingdom, and the United States of America. She received her PhD from the University of Leicester, UK, specializing in International Security and Nuclear Non-proliferation. Previous publications include *Nuclear Deterrence in South Asia: New Technologies and Challenges to Sustainable Peace* (with Zafar Khan, 2019) and *Pakistan and the New Nuclear Taboo: Regional Deterrence and the International Arms Control Regime* (2012).

Innovations in International Affairs
Series Editor: Raffaele Marchetti,
LUISS Guido Carli, Italy

Innovations in International Affairs aims to provide cutting-edge analyses of controversial trends in international affairs with the intent to innovate our understanding of global politics. Hosting mainstream as well as alternative stances, the series promotes both the re-assessment of traditional topics and the exploration of new aspects.

The series invites both engaged scholars and reflective practitioners, and is committed to bringing non-western voices into current debates.

Innovations in International Affairs is keen to consider new book proposals in the following key areas:

- **Innovative topics**: related to aspects that have remained marginal in scholarly and public debates
- **International crises**: related to the most urgent contemporary phenomena and how to interpret and tackle them
- **World perspectives**: related mostly to non-western points of view

Titles in this series include:

States, Civilisations and the Reset of World Order
Richard Higgott

Pivot Cities in the Rise and Fall of Civilizations
Ahmet Davutoğlu
Translated from the Turkish edition by Andrew Boord

Civilizations and World Order
Edited by Elena Chebankova and Piotr Dutkiewicz

Building a Road to Nuclear Disarmament
Bridging the Gap Between Competing Approaches
Rizwana Abbasi

For more information about this series, please visit: https://www.routledge.com/Innovations-in-International-Affairs/book-series/IIA

Building a Road to Nuclear Disarmament

Bridging the Gap Between Competing Approaches

Rizwana Abbasi

Routledge
Taylor & Francis Group

LONDON AND NEW YORK

First published 2022
by Routledge
2 Park Square, Milton Park, Abingdon, Oxon OX14 4RN

and by Routledge
605 Third Avenue, New York, NY 10158

*Routledge is an imprint of the Taylor & Francis Group, an
informa business*

British Library Cataloguing-in-Publication Data
A catalogue record for this book is available from the British
Library

Library of Congress Cataloging-in-Publication Data
Names: Abbasi, Rizwana, 1978- author.
Title: Building a road to nuclear disarmament : bridging
the gap between competing approaches / Rizwana Abbasi.
Description: New York ; Abingdon, Oxon : Routledge,
2022. | Series: Innovations in international affairs | Includes
bibliographical references and index.
Identifiers: LCCN 2021013113 (print) | LCCN 2021013114 (ebook) |
ISBN 9780367673963 (Hardback) | ISBN 9780367673987 (Paperback) |
ISBN 9781003131205 (eBook)
Subjects: LCSH: Nuclear disarmament. | Nuclear arms control. | Nuclear
nonproliferation. | Deterrence (Strategy)
Classification: LCC JZ5665 .A23 2021 (print) | LCC JZ5665 (ebook) |
DDC 327.1/747--dc23 LC record available at https://lccn.loc.gov/
2021013113LC ebook record available at https://lccn.loc.gov/2021013114

ISBN: 978-0-367-67396-3 (hbk)
ISBN: 978-0-367-67398-7 (pbk)
ISBN: 978-1-003-13120-5 (ebk)

DOI: 10.4324/9781003131205

Typeset in Times
by KnowledgeWorks Global Ltd.

Contents

List of abbreviations

A2/AD	Anti-Access Area Denial
AAD	Advanced Air Defence
ABM	Anti-Ballistic Missile Treaty
ANA	Alliance for Nuclear Accountability
ATT	Arms Trade Treaty
BWC	Biological Weapons Convention
CBMs	Confidence Building Measures
CCD	Committee on Disarmament
CCM	Convention on Cluster Munition
CCWC	Convention on Certain Conventional Weapons
CD	Conference on Disarmament
CFE	Conventional Armed Forces in Europe
CND	Campaign for Nuclear Disarmament
CPGS	Conventional Prompt Global Strikes
CSD	Cold Start Doctrine
CTBT	Comprehensive Nuclear Test-Ban Treaty
CWC	Chemical Weapons Convention
DMZ	Demilitarized Zone
DPRK	Democratic People's Republic of Korea
DTTI	Defence Trade Treaty Initiative
END	European Nuclear Disarmament
ENDC	Eighteen Nation Committee on Disarmament
FMCT	Fissile Material Cut-off Treaty
GBSD	Ground Based Strategic Deterrent
GCD	General and Complete Disarmament
GGEs	Group of Government Experts
GPS	Global Prompt Strikes
HGV	Hypersonic Glide Vehicle
ICAN	International Campaign to Abolish Nuclear Weapons
ICBMs	Intercontinental Ballistic Missiles

ICJ	International Court of Justice
ICNND	International Commission on Nuclear Non-Proliferation and Disarmament NPDI Non-proliferation and Disarmament Initiative
ICRC	International Committee of Red Cross
IFRC	International Federation of Red Cross and Red Crescent Societies
IKV	Interchurch Peace Council
INF	Intermediate-Range Nuclear Force Treaty
IOR	Indian Ocean Region
IPPNW	International Physicians for the Prevention of Nuclear War
ISPR	Inter Services Public Relations
ISR	Intelligence, Surveillance and Reconnaissance
JCPOA	Joint Comprehensive Plan of Action
LAC	Line of Actual Control
LAWS	Lethal Autonomous Weapon Systems
LRSO	Long Range Standoff Missile
MIRVs	Multiple Independent Reentry Vehicles
MPI	Middle Powers Initiative
MTCR	Missile Technology Control Regime
NAC	New Agenda Coalition
NAM	Non-Aligned Movement
NAPF	Nuclear Age Peace Foundation
NATO	North Atlantic Treaty Organization
NCBMs	Nuclear Confidence Building Measures
NGOs	Non-Governmental Organizations
NIEO	New International Economic Order
NNWS	Non-Nuclear Weapon States
NPT	Nuclear Non-proliferation Treaty
NPTREC	Non-proliferation Treaty Review and Extension Conference
NRR	Nuclear Restraint Regime
NSG	Nuclear Suppliers Group
NWS	Nuclear Weapon States
OEWG	Open-Ended Working Group
OPCW	Organization for the Prohibition of Chemical Weapons
OPLAN	Operations Plan
OPs	Operational Paragraphs
PAD	Prithvi Air Defence
PTBT	Partial Test Ban Treaty
RMI	Marshall Islands

ROK	Republic of Korea
SALT	Strategic Arms Limitation Treaty
SLBM	Submarine-Launched Ballistic Missiles
SLOCs	Sea Lines of Communications
SORT	Strategic Offensive Reductions Treaty
SSOD-I	Special Session on Disarmament
THAAD	Terminal High Altitude Area Defence
TNCD	Ten-Nation Committee on Disarmament
TPNW	Treaty on the Prohibition of Nuclear Weapons
UAVs	Unmanned Air Vehicles
UNDC	United Nations Disarmament Commission
UNGA	United Nations General Assembly
US	United States
WMD	Weapons of Mass Destruction
WTO	World Trade Organization
ZAC	Zangger Committee

Introduction

This book broadly focuses on comprehending the contemporary global security environment with an aim to create a new road map for nuclear disarmament. This volume narrowly aims at identifying the divide between traditional security-centric aspects and humanity-centred disarmament perspectives while looking into the issues which continue to be obstacles in the way of convincing the nuclear weapon states (NWS) on nuclear disarmament. This book thus tackles the complex question of bridging the divide between competing approaches thereby offering a new road map for nuclear disarmament.

Security-centric approach

The disarmament mandate is already enshrined in the operational paragraphs of the 1968 Nuclear Non-proliferation Treaty (NPT), and in the subsequent measure such as the Indefinite Extension of the NPT (NPTREC) in 1995[1] and the consequent commitments to NPTREC agreed in the NPT Review Conferences in 2000[2] and 2010.[3] The NPTREC gave the clear directives on the strengthening of the review process for the treaty, principles and objectives for nuclear non-proliferation and disarmament (P&O), the extension of the treaty and a resolution on the Middle East.[4] The P&O carried out recommendations and provisions covering all three pillars of the NPT such as nuclear non-proliferation, peaceful uses of nuclear technologies and nuclear disarmament. Furthermore, it was agreed to:[5] (a) complete the negotiation at the Conference on Disarmament (CD) in Geneva of the Comprehensive Nuclear Test-Ban Treaty (CTBT) not later than 1996; (b) immediate commencement and early conclusion of a treaty prohibiting production of fissile material for nuclear weapons (FMCT)[6] and (c) persuasion of systematic and progressive efforts by the NWS to reduce nuclear weapons globally with the ultimate goal of eliminating these arsenals completely.

That said, the NPT Review Conferences in 2000[7] and 2010[8] were widely anticipated as seminal moments for international efforts to achieve nuclear disarmament. Despite a strong emphasis and a forceful pledge to rid the world of nuclear weapons (as prescribed in Article VI of the NPT), little practical progress is made by the NWS on the disarmament agenda. Arguably, it would have been too idealistic to expect meaningful progress on nuclear disarmament given serious underlined concerns of the different groups of the states such as nuclear weapon possessor states and non-nuclear weapon states (NNWS).

Under the NPT, five countries are recognized as NWS – P5 (permanent member of the United Nations Security Council) while the rest of the treaty's signatories are regarded as NNWS. In this equation, after 1968, the international nuclear order established by the NPT[9] allocated the benefits entirely to the five NWS. For instance, Article VI of the NPT highlights that states party to the treaty 'undertake to pursue negotiations in good faith on effective measures relating to cessation of the nuclear arms race at an early date and to nuclear disarmament, and on a treaty on general and complete disarmament.'[10] The NPT Article VI does not legally bind the NWS to eliminate nuclear weapons from their arsenals, but only loosely requires that they start negotiations[11] while non-parties of the NPT have no legal compulsions to commit to the disarmament. This is why, since the adoption of the NPT, the global and regional security environment,[12] despite certain brief interludes of détente[13] when most of the arms limitation and reduction agreements between the United States (US) and Soviet Union (now Russia) were finalized, has not shown any marked progress. Although nuclear arms control negotiations[14] and discussions on crisis management between the US and Soviet Union were set up in the late 1960s while laying down the ground for subsequent arms control treaties such as the Anti-Ballistic Missile Treaty (ABM), Strategic Arms Limitation Treaty (SALT I and II), Intermediate-Range Nuclear Force Treaty (INF) and Strategic Arms Reduction Treaty (START I and II).

Moreover, while the two leading nuclear powers were able to agree on meaningful limits on their nuclear arsenals at the bilateral level to reduce risks of war, they still exhibited tendencies to hedge against possible future contingencies requiring modernizations of nuclear weapons. This was evidenced by the lack of disarmament progress at the multilateral level (UN-led forums) where important treaties such as the CTBT could not enter into force given the non-ratification of two important NWS – China and the US, non-ratification by Egypt, Iran, Israel and the opposition of India, North Korea and Pakistan to sign the treaty. One of the primary stumbling blocks in the way of the effectiveness of the US-led forums, CD has been the differing priorities and preferences of states for individual items on the agenda of the CD, notwithstanding their interlinkages. Each state has endeavoured to promote progress on specific agenda items which are cost-free for them and sought to target the perceived military advantage of the other states. All the treaties and conventions directed to promote non-proliferation of nuclear, biological and chemical weapons and nuclear disarmament lacked coordination with UN conflict resolution mechanisms. Despite strong linkages between conventional and non-conventional technologies, the states failed to introduce a multilateral mechanism to constrain conventional weapons. The existing conventional weapons-related treaties are not synthesized with CD's work on nuclear disarmament. Similarly, biological and chemical convention crisis linked to nuclear disarmament creates power rivalry which marred progress in the past has resurfaced in the present time.

Whereas despite Russia and the US embarked on promising arrangements for arms control and risks reduction following the end of the Cold War, many regions continued to experience conflict and rise in tensions such as the Middle East, Korea Peninsula, South America, Africa and South Asia. Although, the post-Cold War era witnessed some positive developments such as the unilateral destruction of its nuclear weapons by South Africa; the return of Soviet era stationed nuclear weapons in Belarus, Kazakhstan and Ukraine. These states later acceded to the NPT as NNWS. Both Argentina and Brazil also renounced nuclear weapon ambitions and acceded to the NPT as NNWS. In fact, that was the time when in parallel the world witnessed the emergence of another group of the states – four new nuclear weapon possessor states (outside the NPT) such as Israel, India, Pakistan and North Korea. Moreover, several clandestine nuclear weapons programs (actual or alleged), came known to the international community such as North Korea, Iran, Libya and later Syria.

Compared to the era of hope immediately following the demise of the Cold War, the present global and regional security landscapes seem fairly bleak with little prospects for any meaningful move towards nuclear disarmament due to some states' effective deterrent compulsions in the backdrop of renewed great power competition, resurge in global conflicts and states' insecurities. The aggravation of contemporary security situation and growing conventional asymmetries in certain conflict regions such as Asia-Pacific, South Asia, Middle East and Korean peninsula will keep intense security dilemma driven arms racing problem animated between states as underlined below.

The contemporary global political system is entering a multipolar order[15] thereby shifting large and small powers' focus away from the Atlantic and Europe to Asia, thus challenging the relevance[16] of the western-centric non-proliferation treaties. All the existing mechanisms (discussed in the subsequent chapters) directed to promote arms control and disarmament are in despair. Currently, states' reliance on modernization of deterrent force has increased while their emphasis on arms control and disarmament has decreased. These arms racing problems have created dangerous risks of accidental war, miscalculation, problems of strategic instability and disarmament crisis.

That said, emergence of new technologies such as biotechnology,[17] quantum computing and cryptograph, nuclear hypersonic weapons, including hypersonic glide vehicles (HGVs) and hypersonic cruise missiles (HCMs), global prompt strikes (GPS), dominance in space, anti-satellite, surveillance, cyber warfare tools, high energy lasers, artificial intelligence and Lethal Autonomous Weapon Systems (LAWS), low yield nuclear warheads, along with blurring of distinction between low yield nuclear weapons and high-precision advanced conventional munition have lowered the threshold for use of nuclear weapons thereby introducing serious stability challenges for international security in general and stability of broader non-proliferation regime in particular. That said, states such as the US, China, India and Pakistan have undergone an increasing upgradation of existing asymmetries in conventional forces.[18] India is also acquiring new non-nuclear technologies such as missile defence, anti-satellite weapons and conventional counterforce modernization[19] in order to maintain power balance with China or to accomplish status-driven ambitions. States' modernization of nuclear platforms[20] such as upgradation in weapon grade fissile material stockpile, high-technology hardware induction, ballistic missile and force structure, induction of intercontinental ballistic missiles (ICBMs), submarine-launched ballistic missiles (SLBM) and multiple independent reentry vehicles (MIRVs)[21] technologies and surveillance means such as ISR satellites, advanced and smarter air platforms, maritime-based Unmanned Air Vehicle (UAVs), Cruise missile, aircraft carriers and Global Prompt Strikes (GPS), hypersonic and bio-technologies lead to create a destabilizing military advantage in Asia. These arms racing trends have created dangerous risks of accidental war, miscalculations, problems of strategic instability and disarmament crisis in the absence of regulatory frameworks.

The leading technology holders are not willing to discuss any framework for the regulation of the above highlighted technologies.[22] Resultantly, the nuclear possessor states that are competing against regional adversaries in turn become more resistant to the idea of giving up their nuclear options to hedge against the emerging technologies. Besides their potential use for degrading an adversaries' nuclear deterrence, new technologies can provide a decisive conventional edge to the holders of these technologies – this implies more reliance of nuclear weapons by those lacking such technologies.

Allegations of non-compliance with the CTBT by China and Russia and reciprocal allegations by Russia against the US, the demise of the INF Treaty[23] will adversely impact the existing arms control culture. It is due to the fact that the Cold War arms control agreements face double edge dilemma: (a) they do not cover the emerging technologies that will build the next generation weapons and (b) China – a rising power – is not a party to the Cold War time treaties, therefore not constrained in weapons development. Thus, the US aspires to engage both with Russia and China in order to bring the bilateral engagements forward into a trilateral engagement but China persistently resists on a trilateral approach.[24]

The death of the INF Treaty will lead to an arms race between the US and China in the Asia-Pacific. The US withdrawal will lead to dissatisfaction, division and mistrust with its EU partners. Russia's arms build-up and fielding of missile systems will demand a strong North Atlantic Treaty Organization (NATO) response, including renewed nuclear deployments by the EU states. So, the US will be compelled to install more intermediate-range missiles in Europe that in turn would destabilize the broader European region. Poland, the Baltic states and other countries in this part of Europe are concerned about the Russian role to weaken the NATO.[25]

The breakdown of arms control and non-proliferation agreements between the leading nuclear possessor states, and their competition to maximize national security through arms race and dominance, weaken the norms on arms control and restraint, resulting in greater risk prone behaviours at the regional levels without the fear of international reprimand. Discriminatory practices for export control regimes bestowing a sense of entitlement on some states and sidestepping of non-proliferation norms undermine the credibility of non-proliferation regime as a whole which is exploited as a justification for arms race and other risk-prone behaviours.

In sum, renewed tensions between states, the crisis of existing arms control and non-proliferation treaties, rising asymmetries and development of new types of nuclear weapons with new missions and lowered threshold of use, and threats of use of nuclear weapons have brought nuclear deterrent requirements to the forefront and nuclear disarmament to a standstill. Today, follow-on commitments to the 1995 NPTREC agreed in 2000 and 2010 have largely been sidelined. All these above evolving trends between nuclear possessor states have created frustration for NNWS.

A parallel approach

Notwithstanding the above developments, certain countries, frustrated by the progress on nuclear disarmament have come up with a parallel approach focusing on the humanitarian consequences of the use of nuclear weapons and banning them on humanitarian grounds. The history of nuclear weapons cannot be separated from the debates of disarmament which generally emphasize the idea of total elimination of nuclear weapons. Besides state-centric approaches, the global aspiration for a nuclear disarmament has manifested itself in various unilateral, bilateral and multilateral initiatives for a world free of nuclear weapons. The humanitarian approaches for promoting the agenda of a nuclear-free world is fundamentally inherited in the notion of human security contrary to the state-centred view of national security.

That said, in the last decade, new trends have evolved such as development of an unofficial alliance system between NNWS and the non-governmental organizations (NGOs) making efforts jointly to achieve the nuclear-free world. After three successful state-sponsored conferences in Norway, Mexico and Austria focusing on the humanitarian impact of nuclear weapons, in December 2014, the Austrian Government unveiled the 'Humanitarian Pledge' to fill the legal gap for the prohibition and elimination of nuclear weapons.[26] It was initially supported by 127 nations, united in a call to NWS – and those who stand with them – to begin a process leading to nuclear disarmament.[27] Additionally, the International Campaign to Abolish Nuclear Weapons (ICAN), a global coalition of NGOs in over 100 countries was awarded the Nobel Peace Prize in 2017 for its tireless commitments to promote the Treaty on the Prohibition of Nuclear Weapon (TPNW).[28] The global voluntary movements such as green peace[29] and campaign for nuclear disarmament,[30] global zero[31] and other anti-war movements have led to create normative support to the NPT on its nuclear non-proliferation and disarmament agenda. Civil society (discussed in the subsequent chapters) did play a crucial part[32] in promoting disarmament debate at the governmental and public level on range of issues ranging from banning cluster munitions and anti-personnel landmines to implementing the NPT prohibiting nuclear testing.[33] The NGOs and civil society kept the momentum and debates on CTBT[34] thriving and worked closely with government scientists and officials to develop verification solutions and create the conditions that enabled the CD to bring the CTBT to conclusion.[35] Civil society movements[36] also engaged very actively in efforts to promote the elimination of nuclear, chemical and biological arsenals, and in developing and implementing the programme of action on small arms and light weapons. For all these weapons types, civil society has worked both with governments and communities to stigmatize the employment and possession of such weapons.

On the disarmament equation, along with the civil society efforts and the 2017 TPNW adopted by 122 countries (entered into force on 22 January 2021), some other landmark competing approaches that are relevant in the present security environment include the US-led creating the environment for nuclear disarmament (CEND); the Stockholm Initiative on stepping stones to nuclear disarmament advanced by Sweden and 15 other countries in 2018; the humanitarian initiative on the impact of nuclear weapons advanced in 2013 (Norway), 2014 (Mexico and Austria), 2015 (by Austria and 158 other countries); the step-by-step approach to nuclear disarmament advanced by the Group of Non-Aligned States (110 plus NAM States in 2010, 2015 and 2019); the New Agenda Coalition (NAC); the Non-Proliferation and Disarmament Initiative; and the P-5 Process initiated by the United Kingdom in 2008.

Since the NPT Article VI only loosely demands that the NWS start negotiations on disarmament, the 2017 TPNW aimed at strengthening the unimplemented pillar of the NPT. The TPNW and other governmental and non-governmental movements on world free of nuclear weapons fill a gap between nuclear non-proliferation and disarmament while pushing the NWS to abandon nuclear weapons. But TPNW – a normative movement has created frustration and caused controversy and debate between deterrent supporters (NWS) and those who advocate the treaty (NNWS) 'calling its alleged incompatibility with the NPT.'[37] While the TPNW seeks to make nuclear weapons illegal for all countries, while the NPT provided a monopoly on such weapons to the five countries that had proliferated before 1968. The major challenge is that the NWS did not participate in the negotiations of the TPNW, nor did the other states possessing nuclear weapons outside the NPT such as – India, Israel, Pakistan and North Korea.

As the nuclear-weapons states made clear after the treaty was finalized, it is unrealistic in the current international security climate to expect them to eliminate their nuclear weapons. The NWS will not sign the TPNW due to their heavy reliance on nuclear deterrence while nuclear possessor states at the regional level would become insecure with growing asymmetries and continued power gap. Thus the supporters of deterrence believe that TPNW puts necessary strain on the existing nuclear disarmament and non-proliferation process, destabilizing the existing NPT and fragmenting international solidarity of consensus on a world without nuclear weapons. The NWS' deterrent obsession and their passivity towards the treaty, therefore, stimulated grave disappointment as a step backwards from the world without nuclear weapons. In other words, a cursory analysis of the security environments of most NWS will reveal real security concerns and existential threats which will force these states not to renounce nuclear weapons even if strong norms to the contrary evolve.

The first key point here is that the TPNW advocates or the humanitarian consequences groups fail to build the strong link between security and progress on disarmament. Such strong linkage between security and progress on disarmament has been acknowledged by the First Special Session of the UN General Assembly on Disarmament (SSOD-I, 1978). There was consensus among the international community that disarmament has to be non-discriminatory and proportional with leading nuclear weapons holders taking the lead. Moreover, at every step of the disarmament process, it has to be ensured that no state or a group of states acquires a military advantage over the others and that equal and undiminished security for all states has to be guaranteed.

Further key point here is that the civil society and states sponsored disarmament advocators of the TPNW base their idea on the humanitarian impact, but they potentially fail to build the interface of new challenges of emerging advanced technologies for nuclear weapons policies and doctrines, and the resulting impact on nuclear arms race and nuclear disarmament. The TPNW itself was perceived by the civil society groups and the public alike as major leap forward to a world without nuclear weapons; although, this treaty will create irreconcilable political cleavage between those who advocate it and those who hold monopoly on nuclear weapons. The TPNW may not be equipped with power to bridge the gap between NWS and NNWS unless it incorporates debates on emerging tensions at the regional level, states security demands, thereby building the interface of new challenges of emerging advanced technologies for nuclear weapons policies and doctrines, and the resulting impact on nuclear arms racing and nuclear disarmament.

Bridging the gap between the two approaches

Thus there is need to bridge the gap between NWS and NNWS by creating balance between states' security needs and disarmament. The serious question arises how should we maintain balance between some states' aspirations for disarmament and other states' need for an effective nuclear deterrent for their national security? The norm against nuclear weapons, in the absence of any nuclear weapon possessor state joining the TPNW, it is not likely to lead to a practical ban on nuclear weapons until certain new conditions set and the new security environment created to address states disparities and differences.

New approaches must be considered keeping in view the emergence of new kind of risks, especially in relation to emerging technologies and their impact on strategic stability and disarmament. The risks posed by new technologies, especially the possibility of conventional entanglement which result in greater risks in the nuclear field, warrants closer attention. Multilateral discourse on regulating the holistic use of new technologies and their militarization has not kept pace with the advancement in such technologies. There is an urgent need for developing clarity and understandings on a multilateral regulatory framework and further development of international norms and legally binding agreements for avoiding the employment of new technologies in a manner that can threaten deterrence stability and disarmament prospects. Certain risks reduction measures that have worked in the past, or those that have proven to be useful bilaterally or between specific states, might not be effective in the contemporary context involving a different set of players and new forms of weapons systems and enabling technologies. It would be worthwhile to look at a new framework for risk reduction which is holistic and integrated and include risks reduction across various domains including conventional, nuclear and emerging technologies, whether they are specifically weaponized or not.

The book will broadly fill this gap highlighted above in the intellectual and policy discourses thereby offering a way forward creating balance between states' security needs and disarmament. This book tackles the complex question how tension between emerging technologies and TPNW be resolved? How balance between some states' short-term requirements for effective nuclear deterrence and other states long-term desire for nuclear-free world be created? This book offers lessons on how effectively divide between traditional security-centric and human-centred approaches be bridged?

Core argument of the book

The core argument is that the divide between traditional security-centric aspects and human-centred perspective has widened, which in turn has marginalized prospects for nuclear disarmament. The study argues that divide between competing approaches can be bridged by creating new security environment. The norm against nuclear weapons is not likely to lead to a practical ban on nuclear weapons until certain new conditions set and the new security environment created to address states' disparities and differences. Thus, without serious and meaningful work in the UN system for proactive security mechanism which proves guarantees for states against arbitrary action by militarily powerful states, it will not be easy to convince states to give up nuclear weapons. For that purpose, revival of CD to negotiate nuclear disarmament as a part of comprehensive programme of work which provides for simultaneous effort to address non-nuclear military asymmetries, militarization of nuclear technologies, prevention of arms race in out space by using the framework offered by the SSOD-I will assist in creation of a new security environment to build a new road to disarmament.

What is different, more innovative and better about the book?

This book is different and innovative in multiple ways, that is, most of the work and literature covered on disarmament is part of the history. The present volume goes beyond the pessimistic disarmament narrative to analysing the emerging and future security architecture in light of the contemporary key literature on the subject which in turn reflects disarmament debate as the central focus of the global nuclear politics. Based on the contemporary policy level developments, this book offers a future security mechanism/cooperation amid broken alliance system and crisis of arms control to promote peace and achieve disarmament which in turn makes this volume interesting and innovative. This book makes a unique combination of various essential issues knit together to understand what the contemporary challenging nuclear environment stands for and why it is more important to the world in order to understand the nuclear disarmament prospects. This book then offers a renewed mechanism to build a new road to achieve disarmament in the 21st century by bridging gap between three groups of states such as NWS, NNWS and Non-NPT NWS.

This book is timely, rigorous and futuristic as it offers new voice and diversity of opinions to the plurality of existing viewpoints based on exploratory research method. Thus, in addition to the large amount of secondary and tertiary sources consulted for this work, it is also based on key interviews and personal observations by attending various key national and international seminars/conferences/talks, etc.

This study would capture the attention of a bigger audience interested in security studies, strategic studies, nuclear policy, deterrence thinking, proliferation/non-proliferation aspects of nuclear weapons programme, etc. This book also becomes relevant for academic community, policymakers, diplomatic community, universities, to the members of NGOs, professional research institutes and organizations working in this area.

Organization of the chapters

The introduction of this book presents the broader structure and opens up the main theme of the proposed volume discussing contemporary evolving global security environment and its impact on nuclear disarmament. The book looks into the issues which continue to be obstacles in the way of convincing the NWS on nuclear disarmament. The book unravels the gap between competing approaches such as traditional security-centric aspects and humanity-centred disarmament perspectives and identifies need for a fresh mechanism to build a new road to nuclear disarmament.

Chapter 1 builds understanding on different strands of the non-proliferation regime building comparative analysis as to why some of the instruments of the regime have proven to be successful while others remained ineffective. It seeks to develop understanding on how lack of transparency in some of the regimes led to create crisis of trust between NWS and NNWS, thereby affecting the progress on nuclear disarmament.

Chapter 2 builds a debate on other competing approaches to disarmament such as humanitarian campaigns at the grassroots, civil society movements and coalition of states to promote total elimination of nuclear weapons. While recounting the contribution of the humanitarian initiatives in keeping the disarmament agenda alive and reinvigorating it, the chapter looks into the issues which continue to be obstacles in the way of convincing the NWS on nuclear disarmament.

Chapter 3 discusses contemporary global security environment covering ground on renewed great power competition, resurgence of inter-state rivalries, increasing weapons asymmetries and states' evolving military doctrines. The chapter argues that the shifting centres of powers, evolving global and regional alliances, and intensified inter-state conflicts have aggravated weapon asymmetries. As states' reliance on nuclear weapons and other new technologies increases, their political will to pursue arms control and risks reduction mechanism through cooperation decreases thereby making a road to nuclear disarmament difficult. The chapter investigates why is the influence of nuclear weapons technologies on international security affairs so pervasive? Why has states' reliance on nuclear weapons and new technologies increased while their effort towards disarmament decreased?

Chapter 4 focuses on bridging the divide between competing approaches on nuclear disarmament. This chapter finds out answer to key questions how divergent views can be converged meaningfully to find a common ground where security for every state is guaranteed and nuclear disarmament goal accomplished in line with the Article VI of the NPT? This chapter offers a renewed mechanism to build a new road to nuclear disarmament.

In the concluding section, the book takes forward the major arguments and the analytical issues highlighted in the preceding chapters. This section confirms that by creating new security environment, a visible road to nuclear disarmament can be built. This chapter proves that by adopting multipronged, step-by-step global and regional approaches the gaps between competing approaches be reduced and a new environment created for nuclear disarmament. The suggested arrangements in this book will lead to preserve arms control culture, thereby making the non-proliferation regimes consistent to achieve nuclear disarmament.

Notes

1. See Jayantha Dhanapala, 'The Permanent Extension of the NPT, 1995,' in Andrew F. Cooper, Jorge Heine, and Ramesh Thakur (eds.), *The Oxford Handbook of Modern Diplomacy* (Oxford: Oxford University Press, 2013); also see Tariq Rauf and Rebecca Johnson, 'After the NPT's Indefinite Extension: The Future of the Global Nonproliferation Regime,' *Nonproliferation Review*, Vol. 3, No. 1 (Fall 1995), pp. 28–42: https://doi.org/10.1080/10736709508436604.
2. Tariq Rauf, 'An Unequivocal Success? Implications of the NPT Review Conference,' *Arms Control Association* (July/August 2000): https://www.armscontrol.org/act/2000-07/features/unequivocal-success-implications-npt-review-conference.

3. See Tariq Rauf, '25 Years After the Indefinite Extension of the Nuclear Non-Proliferation Treaty: A Field of Broken Promises and Shattered Visions,' *In Depth News* (May 11, 2020): https://www.indepthnews.net/index.php/opinion/3529-25-years-after-the-indefinite-extension-of-the-nuclear-non-proliferation-treaty-a-field-of-broken-promises-and-shattered-visions.
4. Ibid.
5. Ibid.
6. Daryl Kimball, 'Fissile Material Cut-off Treaty (FMCT) at a Glance,' *Arms Control Association* (June 2018): https://www.armscontrol.org/factsheets/fmct.
7. Tariq Rauf, 'The 2000 NPT Review Conference,' *The Nonproliferation Review,* Vol. 7, No. 1 (February 5, 2008), pp. 146–161.
8. Deepti Choubey, 'Understanding the 2010 NPT Review Conference,' *Carnegie Endowment for International Peace* (June 03, 2010): https://carnegieendowment.org/2010/06/03/understanding-2010-npt-review-conference-pub-40910.
9. William Walker, 'Nuclear Order and Disorder,' International *Affairs,* Vol. 76, No. 4 (Oct., 2000), pp. 703–724.
10. See 'Treaty on the Non-Proliferation of Nuclear Weapons (NPT),' *Office for Disarmament Affairs, United Nations*: https://www.un.org/disarmament/wmd/nuclear/npt/text/.
11. John Carlson, 'Is the NPT Still Relevant? – How to Progress the NPT's Disarmament Provisions,' *Journal for Peace and Nuclear Disarmament*, Vol. 2, No. 1, (2019), pp. 97–113.
12. See William C. Potter and Gaukhar Mukhatzhanova (eds.), *Forecasting Nuclear Proliferation in the 21st Century: A Comparative Perspective*, Volume 2 (Stanford: Stanford University Press, 2010).
13. Paul H. Nitz, 'Assuring Strategic Stability in an Era of Détente,' *Foreign Affairs,* Vol. 54, No. 2 (January 1976), pp. 207–232.
14. See Paolo Foradori, Giampiero Giacomello and Alessandro Pascolini (eds.), *Arms Control and Disarmament: 50 Years of Experience in Nuclear Education* (Cham, Switzerland: Palgrave MacMillan, 2018).
15. Gilford J. Ikenberry, 'From Hegemony to the Balance of Power: The Rise of China and American Grand Strategy in East Asia,' *International Journal of Korean Unification Studies*, Vol. 23, No. 2 (2014), pp. 41–63.
16. Robert Einhorn, 'Non-Proliferation Challenges Facing the Trump Administration,' *Foreign Policy at Brooking, Arms Control and Non-Proliferation Series Paper* 15 (March 2017): https://www.brookings.edu/research/non-proliferation-challenges-facing-the-trump-administration/.
17. Francisco Galamas, 'Biotechnology and Biological Weapons: Challenges to the U.S. Regional Stability Strategy,' *Comparative Strategy*, Vol. 28, No. 2, pp. 164–169.
18. Rizwana Abbasi and Zafar Khan, *Nuclear Deterrence in South Asia: New Technologies and Challenges to Sustainable Peace* (London and New York: Routledge, 2019).
19. Christopher Clary and Vipin Narang, 'India's Counterforce Temptations,' *International Security,* Vol. 43, No. 3 (Winter 2018/19), pp. 7–52; See Toby Dalton and George Perkovich, 'India's Nuclear Options and

Escalation Dominance,' *Carnegie Endowment for International Peace* (May 19, 2016): https://carnegieendowment.org/2016/05/19/india-s-nuclear-options-and-escalation-dominance-pub-63609; See Michael Krepon, 'The Counterforce Compulsion in South Asia,' *Arms Control Wonk* (April 12, 2017): https://www.armscontrolwonk.com/archive/1203018/the-counterforce-compulsion-in-south-asia/; See Shivshankar Menon, *Choices: Inside the Making of India's Foreign Policy* (Washington: Brookings Institution Press, 2016); Shashank Joshi, 'An Evolving India Nuclear Doctrine?,' in Michael Krepon, Joshua T. White, Julia Thomson and Shane Mason (eds.), *Deterrence Instability and Nuclear Weapons in South Asia* (Washington, DC: Stimson Center, 2015), p. 93.

20. Abbasi and Khan, *Nuclear Deterrence in South Asia: New Technologies and Challenges to Sustainable Peace*.

21. See Michael Krepon, Travis Wheeler and Shane Mason (eds.), *The Lure and Pitfalls of MIRVS: From first to the Second Nuclear Age* (Washington D.C: Stimson, 2016).

22. Although Russia has indicated its willingness to include new delivery systems in New START extension discussions while US has not responded as yet.

23. See 'The Post-INF Treaty Crisis: Background and Next Steps,' *The Arms Control Association* Vol. 11, No. 8 (August 7, 2019): https://www.armscontrol.org/issue-briefs/2019-08/post-inf-treaty-crisis-background-next-steps.

24. Kingston Reif and Shannon Bugos, 'Trump Still Wants Multilateral Arms Control,' *Arms Control Association* (April 2020): https://www.armscontrol.org/act/2020-04/news/trump-still-wants-multilateral-arms-control.

25. Judy Dempsey, 'Europe and the End of the INF Treaty,' *Carnegie Europe* (February 05, 2019): https://carnegieeurope.eu/strategiceurope/78284.

26. Rebecca Johnson, 'Civil Society and the Conference on Disarmament,' *UNIDIR Resources* (February 2011), pp. 1–5: https://unidir.org/publication/civil-society-and-conference-disarmament.

27. See 'Civil Society Engagement in Disarmament Processes: The Case for a Nuclear Weapons Ban,' *United Nations Publication* (2016): https://www.un.org/disarmament/wp-content/uploads/2017/03/civil-society-2016.pdf.

28. Motoko Mekata, 'How Transnational Civil Society Realized the Ban Treaty: An Interview with Beatrice Fihn,' *Journal for Peace and Nuclear Disarmament*, Vol. 1, No. 1 (2018), pp. 79–92.

29. Bunny McDiarmid, 'Nuclear Testing Is Not a Path to Security and Peace,' *GreenPeace* (August 29, 2016): https://www.greenpeace.org/international/story/7288/nuclear-testing-is-not-a-path-to-security-and-peace/.

30. See 'Campaign for Nuclear Disarmament': https://cnduk.org/.

31. See 'Global Zero, A World without Nuclear Weapons': https://www.globalzero.org/.

32. Mushtapha K. Pasha and David L. Blaney, 'Elusive Paradise: The Promise and Peril of Global Civil Society,' *Alternatives*, Vol. 23, No. 4 (1998), p. 420.

33. Johnson, 'Civil Society and the Conference on Disarmament,' pp. 1–5.

34. Rebecca Johnson, *Unfinished Business: The Negotiation of the CTBT and the End of Nuclear Testing* (New York and Geneva: United Nations, 2009): https://www.unidir.org/files/publications/pdfs/unfinished-business-the-negotiation-of-the-ctbt-and-the-end-of-nuclear-testing-346.pdf.
35. Johnson, 'Civil Society and the Conference on Disarmament,' pp. 1–6.
36. Ann M. Florini (ed.), *The Third Force: The Rise of Transnational Civil Society* (Washington DC: Carnegie Endowment for International Peace, 2000).
37. Tytti Eraso, 'The NPT and TPNW: Compatible or Conflicting Nuclear Weapons Treaties,' *SIPRI* (March 2019): https://www.sipri.org/commentary/blog/2019/npt-and-tpnw-compatible-or-conflicting-nuclear-weapons-treaties.

1 Nuclear disarmament
Tracing lessons from history

Introduction

The development of nuclear weapons by the United States (US), their use during the World War-II and further, proliferation led to generate extensive deliberations in the political and academic circles on the nature and role of nuclear weapons and concept of deterrence. American think tanks such as RAND and renowned scholars such as Brodie,[1] Shelling[2] and Wohlstetter[3] made sizeable contribution to understand the importance of these weapons in war and peace times. Thus, the concept of deterrence was broadly discussed in the US strategic thinking, which correspondingly assisted the US and the former Soviet Union (now Russia) to develop their doctrinal plans, craft contingency strategies, deliberate on budgetary questions and understand significance of the arms negotiations. It can therefore be argued that the nuclear deterrence debate ushered in acceptance for nuclear weapons, which thus became a vital policy tool of some states' national security. So, deterrence theory[4] endeavoured to invert the normative association between deterrence and disarmament by asserting that nuclear weapons maintain peace and prevent war rather than promoting it.

Concurrent to the deterrence debate, efforts were being undertaken to legalize the prohibition on the proliferation, possession and employment of nuclear weapons.[5] Subsequently, Nuclear Non-proliferation Regime evolved as a broad construct, comprising different treaties, conventions and arrangements, which assembled states to promote non-proliferation of nuclear weapons, arms control and disarmament. Some of these instruments are more formal while others are in the form of concurred guidelines that members accept or opt to disregard. The principles and values of the broader non-proliferation regime are: (a) to promote global peace and stability through cooperation and

DOI: 10.4324/9781003131205-1

trust building; (b) to achieve security through restraint and not dominance; (c) to promote concept of shared security through compromises and (d) to promote rules-based criteria to achieve undiminished security for all.

More narrowly, in the field of nuclear non-proliferation, the NPT led to promote multilateral arrangements to limit the horizontal spread of all types of nuclear weapons including some of the conventional technologies. Arguably, states focus remained more on non-proliferation while less on disarmament.

In the arms control field, the paramount consideration was reduction of risks of a nuclear war and maintaining deterrence stability than the pursuit of genuine measures that could ultimately lead to the goal of nuclear disarmament. Most arms control agreements and arrangements related to the two superpowers, i.e. the US and Soviet Union (now Russia) with a few exceptions, there existed no multilateral forums on arms reduction at a global level. Although the arms control negotiations introduced stability between the US and Soviet Union but failed to build any impetus for disarmament debate. Even though, the nuclear disarmament deliberations evolved in parallel, on the UN forums (as discussed below), nevertheless states failed to come to consensus on the total elimination of nuclear weapons because of their political differences and nonexistence of treaty-based multilateral legal mechanism.

Sketching guiding posts from the above description, this chapter thematically builds three sections to explain the dynamics attached to nuclear disarmament process. The discussion in the leading section assesses the treaties that are aimed to promote non-proliferation of WMDs and conventional technologies and their impact on trust building process between NWS and NNWS on disarmament. The second section generates a debate on bilateral arms control arrangements between the US and Soviet Union, their effectiveness and impact on strategic stability and disarmament debate. The third section presents a holistic discussion on the UN-led disarmament forums asking why these forums failed to create a consensus on total elimination of nuclear weapons and that how failure of the disarmament process led to impact stability of the broader non-proliferation regime. Finally, this chapter draws lessons as to how some regimes had proven to be effective while other arrangements led to promote a crisis of trust between NWS and NNWS, thereby impacting states' consensus to construct a clear road to disarmament.

Non-proliferation and disarmament of biological and chemical weapons and conventional arms control

This section examines the treaties and conventions relating to nuclear non-proliferation and evaluates the effectiveness or ineffectiveness of the treaties asking why these instruments failed to achieve global consensus on disarmament. It then goes on to briefly overview the conventions and treaties related to disarmament and non-proliferation of biological, chemical and conventional weapons insofar as it is necessary to explore the linkages between nuclear disarmament and other categories of weapons asking how crisis in the nuclear order impacts the regimes related to other types of weapons and vice versa.

Non-proliferation: NPT-centric order affecting the disarmament process

The first institutional attempt to promote norms against proliferation of nuclear material was made with the establishment of the International Atomic Energy Agency (IAEA) in 1957. The rationale was to promote the peaceful uses of nuclear energy while ensuring 'assistance provided by the IAEA or at its request, or under its supervision or control is not used in such a way as to further any military purpose.'[6] The IAEA established its Safeguards system to verify the non-diversion of nuclear materials, services, equipment, facilities and information made available by the agency from peaceful uses to military purposes. In addition to verifying non-diversion commitments of recipients of nuclear technologies under the IAEA auspices, the statute also provided for application of Safeguards, at the request of the parties, to any bilateral or multilateral arrangement, or at the request of a state, to any of that state's activities in the field of atomic energy.[7]

Later, the NPT came into force in 1970, with a range of obligations for NWS and NNWS.[8] It was established with the conviction that the proliferation of nuclear weapons would augment the threat of a nuclear war. Thus, the treaty required NWS not to transfer nuclear weapons or other nuclear explosives or control over such devices or assistance to NNWS (Article I). The treaty envisages the NNWS not to acquire, manufacture or seek assistance in the manufacturing of nuclear weapons or explosive devices (Article II). The treaty limited the number of NWS to the US, Russia, France, the United Kingdom and China. The rest of the states, party to the treaty relinquished the nuclear weapon option and in return received two commitments, i.e., the inalienable right to nuclear energy (Article IV) and an obligation on the part of NWS to end the arms race and dismantle their nuclear arsenals (Article VI). The treaty also gives party states the right to withdrawal by giving a three-month notice. Finally, the treaty also had provisions for review conferences to be held at five-year intervals and for an extension conference to be held 25 years after the treaty entered into force, to decide by a majority vote whether the treaty should be extended indefinitely, or not at all.

After it came into force, the NPT assigned the IAEA the responsibility of verifying its Safeguards system at the global level. Under Article IV.2 and Article III of the NPT, the IAEA verifies the implementation of non-proliferation obligations.[9] Additionally, some other important informal measures had been introduced to strengthen the NPT norms and assist in coordination among its member states. In 1974, an intergovernmental group reckoned as Zangger Committee (ZAC) was established as the 'faithful interpreter' of the NPT Article III.2 (aimed at reaching a common understanding on the definition of equipment or material especially designed or prepared for the processing, use or production of special fissionable material and the conditions and procedures that would govern the exports of such equipment or material), to harmonize the interpretation of nuclear export control policies for NPT parties. Subsequently, the Nuclear Supplier Group (NSG) later renamed from its original name London Group (an offshoot of the NPT) emerged in response to 1974 Indian explosions with the purpose of halting the further proliferation of nuclear weapons. The aim was to reinforce the NPT's Article III and IV to ascertain that transfer of nuclear material would not be diverted to unsafeguarded nuclear fuel cycles and nuclear explosive activities. Moreover, Missile Technology Control Regime (MTCR) and Wassenaar Arrangement (WA) were introduced to ensure regulation of the ballistic missiles and other unmanned delivery systems that could be employed for chemical, biological and nuclear attacks and conventional arms and dual-use technologies, respectively. These informal measures had been introduced to strengthen the NPT norms and facilitate coordination among its member states.

Commenting on the NPT construct, Futter argued, 'The NPT was setup with more of a focus on anti-proliferation rather disarmament, reflecting the geopolitical realities of the late 1960s. In terms of disarmament, the problem has always been a reluctance on the part of the five recognized nuclear weapons states to fully disarm, and of course the fact that four more nuclear armed states now reside outside the treaty.'[10] The NPT-based construct, elucidated above, had proven to be partially successful in order to attain nuclear non-proliferation goals, whereas failed to make advancement on nuclear disarmament. For example, while focusing on its successes, President Kennedy's prediction in 1963 that 15–20 states would get nuclear weapons by 1964[11] has not yet come to pass. The underlined features determine that the NPT somehow played a central role to stabilize the global nuclear order. Firstly, since inception, the NPT's membership (currently 191) has strengthened the nuclear non-proliferation process.

Secondly, majority of the countries – the NNWS – are steadfast to not manufacture nuclear weapons, including states like South Africa, Brazil and Argentina which once possessed or considered to procure nuclear weapons renounced it and subsequently joined the NPT as NNWS. Nearly, 110 NNWS party to the nuclear-weapon-free zones have accepted legal obligations not to build or possess/control any nuclear explosive devices on their territories. Although it was a voluntary choice of these countries to stay nuclear-free due to their belief that nuclear weapons cause destruction, these states' adherence to the NPT added value to the credibility of the treaty. Additionally, some voluntary movements such as anti-war movements and humanitarian initiatives (discussed in the subsequent chapter) on disarmament have led to create normative support to the NPT on its nuclear non-proliferation goals.

Despite its successes, the NPT is under deep stress due to the following reasons. Firstly, under the NPT, only five signatories are considered as recognized NWS, while the rest are regarded as NNWS and are barred from acquiring nuclear weapons. This special arrangement legitimizes the continuous possession of nuclear weapons by five NWS and endorses disarmament of the unarmed states which creates a deep division between NWS and NNWS. Secondly, while placing the obligation on NWS to stop the nuclear arms race, and eventually abolish the nuclear weapons completely, Article VI of the NPT fails to specify the exact timeline or a verification mechanism on disarmament. Some view the stationing of nuclear warheads by NWS on the territories of NNWS states as violation of article obligation of NWS. This evidently overburdened NNWS for upholding their obligations to non-proliferation instead of putting emphasis on NWS for their commitments to disarm. Such noticeable perception has led to prove that the NPT is principally focused on preserving the interests of the P-5 states and that has raised global criticism on the regime's discriminatory construct.

Third, challenge relates to the treaty's non-universality, that is, India, Israel and Pakistan (nuclear possessor states) have never joined the NPT. India (tested nuclear devices first in 1974 and later in 1998) and Pakistan (followed the Indian tests in 1998) developed nuclear arsenals and declared themselves to be NWS, while Israel has maintained the policy of 'nuclear opacity' since 1968. After 1968, when NPT allocated benefits entirely to the five NWS, India also asked for a fair share of power within the international nuclear order. The challenge of universality was further deepened by North Korea, which previously joined the NPT but later withdrew in 2003 and tested nuclear devices many times since 2006 despite global sanctions.[12] The NPT is under serious pressure in the backdrop of North Korean behaviour,[13] particularly after the detonation of its hydrogen bomb and induction of ICBMs.[14] There have been lingering concerns that North Korea's behaviour may threaten states like South Korea and Japan, with advanced nuclear weapons development capabilities to opt for nuclear deterrence. In the case of such concerns translating into reality, the NPT regime could lose its worth. Iran presents yet another challenge to the NPT. In the backdrop of the US withdrawal from the Joint Comprehensive Plan of Action (JCPOA), agreement and subsequent steps taken by Iran[15] inconsistent with the JCPOA thresholds, Iran might follow the North Korean steps while creating further dent for the NPT. Andrew said, 'there are nine nuclear weapons states which do not want to give up nuclear weapons for their security or other reasons while four of them do not adhere to the treaty which indeed is more problematic and makes disarmament a distant dream.'[16]

The fourth set of challenge to the NPT-centric order arises from the absence of formal arrangements in relation to Article III.2 of the NPT. In the absence of specificity in the NPT with regard to such a mechanism, the task of defining the conditions and procedures governing nuclear exports has been assumed by the NSG. As the name suggests, it is an informal grouping of 48 nuclear supplier states, which excludes the majority of NNWS parties to the NPT. Regardless of states' compliance with their IAEA Safeguards obligations, states can be subjected to denials or restrictions in terms of access to nuclear technology based on the strategic or commercial priorities of the technology suppliers. A case in point has been Iran, which officially cited unjust denials from supplier states as a reason for its clandestine procurements from the oversight of the IAEA. The 2008 waiver granted by the NSG to India, whereby India was exempted from the comprehensive safeguards conditionality for nuclear trade in the NSG guidelines, raised questions regarding rule-based conduct of the NSG. India, a non-NPT NWS, in addition to operating unsafeguarded nuclear weapons-related facilities, has not placed its eight civilian power generation reactors under the IAEA Safeguards and has also sought to keep its fast breeder reactor outside international scrutiny.

There is also a serious question mark on India's adherence to the Additional Protocol.[17] Importantly, the agency cannot monitor the research and development activities without the protocol. Within the conditions of the Model Additional Protocol on sharing the activities and facilities with the IAEA, India only agreed to submit information on nuclear-related exports. India does not report information on nuclear fuel cycle-related research and development, nuclear-related imports and uranium mining. Considering its ambitions to build a secret nuclear city to expand and modernize its programme,[18] operationalization of a triad and induction of long-range missiles (discussed in the subsequent chapters), India pursues implicit nuclear activities outside of the safeguards. Despite these realities, the group members have created provision to offer India the benefits of an NPT state.[19] Such provision ridicules the legitimacy and efficacy of the NPT-centric non-proliferation order.

Finally, a set of challenges also emanate from the unimplemented decisions of the NPT extension and post-extension conference. For example, at the 1995 NPT review and extension conference, member states accepted to indefinitely extend the treaty based on a set of decisions that included P&O for nuclear non-proliferation and disarmament. These decisions called for a CTBT, negotiations on a verifiable treaty banning the production of fissile material for nuclear weapons, and for 'systematic and progressive efforts to reduce nuclear weapons globally.'[20] The P-5 countries, as NWS sought indefinite extension in the NPT. The Nuclear Age Peace Foundation, as well as dozens of other civil society groups (discussed in the subsequent chapter) working on nuclear disarmament,[21] particularly those that favoured arms control measures over disarmament, supported the position of the NWS. These civil society groups also observed lack of effort and progress by NWS in fulfilling their Article VI commitments.[22] Therefore, civil society groups exerted pressure on NWS to stop ignoring obligations under the treaty and favoured periodic extensions to be contingent upon clear progress towards nuclear disarmament made by the nuclear-armed parties to the treaty.[23] In the end, the delegates adopted an indefinite extension by consensus. The discussion also included the resolution drafted by the US, the United Kingdom and Russia on the Middle East calling for all states in the region to accede to the NPT (i.e., Israel) and work towards the 'establishment of an effectively verifiable Middle East zone free of weapons of mass destruction.'[24] In nearly a quarter-century since then, this resolution yielded no positive dividends but frustration for the Arab states, and Israel remains the only nuclear possessor states in the Middle East. This was a missed prospect as occurred at the particular crossroads of the NPT in the post-Cold War era when there was a real opening to put pressure on the NWS to fulfil their nuclear disarmament obligations.

The 2000 NPT Review Conference, laid out 13 steps towards nuclear disarmament, including an 'unequivocal undertaking by the NWS to accomplish the total elimination of their nuclear arsenals.'[25] This was significant move in the sense that it re-committed NWS to the Article VI obligations, and for the first time in the NPT's history, the NWS agreed to 'the total elimination of their nuclear arsenals.'[26] This success was the outcome of tough negotiations between the P-5 and the New NAC, which included Brazil, Egypt, Ireland, Mexico, New Zealand, South Africa and Sweden. Subsequently, the political environment shifted and the Bush Administration rejected the US commitments including the CTBT and the agreed 13-step agenda that led to an abject failure of the 2005 NPT Review Conference, with no agreement on implementation of the treaty effectively.

In 2010, the US President, Barack Obama laid down a clear ground for the 2010 NPT Review Conference. He intended to strengthen the international law and established security regimes to prevent the spread of nuclear, biological and chemical weapons, following his Prague speech,[27] President Obama undertook range of initiatives including convening a special session of the United Nations Security Council (UNSC) heads of governments in September 2009 that adopted resolution 1887 on nuclear non-proliferation, signing the New START Treaty with Russia, reducing the role of nuclear weapons in the US national security policy, and getting 47 key states together for the series of nuclear security summits. Widely considered a success, the final outcome document[28] of the 2010 NPT Review Conference included a 64-item action plan covering the NPT's three pillars (discussed above) and a commitment to implement the 1995 Resolution on the Middle East. While NWS opposed, many NNWS, and mainly the non-aligned states, strongly supported the idea of negotiating a nuclear weapons convention that would delegitimize nuclear weapons and eliminate them within a clear timeframe.

The 2015 NPT Review Conference was unsuccessful in producing a final outcome document due to deep divisions between the NWS and NNWS. The most contentious issues were nuclear disarmament and discussions of a Middle East WMD-Free Zone. Importantly, humanitarian approach to nuclear disarmament drew a wide range of support but was also a source of tension and disagreement. In the end, the disagreement over convening a conference on a Middle East WMD-Free Zone prevented the review conference from adopting a final document.[29]

The above facts suggest that today the entire non-proliferation regime is widely considered as a system in distress. The NWS and NNWS are totally divided on total elimination of nuclear weapons. The parallel initiatives listed above aimed at strengthening the NPT norms and facilitate coordination among its member states failed to achieve their goals. The P-5 states not only influenced all the review conferences but also made their implementation difficult which in turn made a road to disarmament difficult.

Non-proliferation and disarmament of biological and chemical weapon

The UN-based protocols such as Biological Weapons Convention (BWC)[30] and Chemical Weapons Convention (CWC)[31] are the most comprehensive, inclusive and non-discriminatory treaties that promote nuclear non-proliferation and disarmament of biological and chemical weapons.

The BWC effectively prohibits the development, production, acquisition, transfer, stockpiling and use of biological and toxin weapons along with equipment, and delivery vehicles designed to such agents or toxins for hostile purposes or in armed conflicts. The BWC is a durable and first multilateral disarmament treaty, banning an entire category of weapons of mass destruction in the field. The BWC is not an isolated instrument, rather it is also related to other ongoing global initiatives of international security, such as global health security and non-proliferation. The interconnection of global initiatives like this reinforces all of the initiatives. The Global Health Security Agenda,[32] for instance, gets 55 states together to strengthen countries' capacities to prevent, detect and respond to infectious disease threats, whether natural, deliberate or accidental. It recognizes that the issue of infectious disease has both a health and biosecurity component. The ties between the goals of the BWC and those of other relevant initiatives make the BWC, in the view of some states, a logical and relevant platform. These are positive signs not only for the role the BWC plays in prohibiting the development and use of biological weapons – including the application of the BWC to new biotechnological advances – but also to the future importance of the BWC in the larger global security architecture.

Similarly, the CWC is another multilateral treaty that bans chemical weapons and required their destruction within a specified period of time. The treaty is of unlimited duration and is far more comprehensive than the 1925 Geneva protocol, which outlaws the use but not the possession of chemical weapons. The CWC was implemented by the Organization for the Prohibition of Chemical Weapon (OPCW). The significance of this treaty is that it prohibits development, production, acquisition, stockpile, transfer, retention, use or military preparation for use of chemical weapons.

Both the treaties promote a stringent export control system and prohibit the possession of biological and chemical weapons by anyone state without discrimination. These are real-time effective and non-discriminatory treaties and protocols that promote rules-based criteria. These are unbiased arrangements that carried a roadmap and inclusive mechanism for non-proliferation and disarmament of biological and chemical weapons. These protocols introduced effective international verification system and they have worked well till date. In this sense, these protocols are interconnected to nuclear disarmament process.

States do not challenge the efficacy and legitimacy of these treaties but some of the states have held back verification, citing[33] continued retention of nuclear weapons by NWS. Some states didn't sign these treaties because they relate their non-ratification on CWC with possession of nuclear weapons with regional countries. For example, five states have neither signed nor acceded to the convention: Angola, Egypt, North Korea, Somalia and Syria. Two states have signed the treaty but not ratified it: Israel and Myanmar. Egypt relates its security rationale to Israel signing the NPT.[34] Syria considers its possession of chemical weapons as a necessary security asset in the backdrop of strategic imbalance in conventional military forces between Israel and Syria.[35] Politics of CWC on Syria case[36] leads to undermining of international confidence with blaming on nuclear disarmament prospects. Thus, security concerns of these states need to be taken into consideration.

However, in recent years, it seems that there is increased politicization of the OPCW[37] in parallel with new strategic competition between global powers (discussed in the subsequent chapters). The present global security environment (discussed in the subsequent chapters) has created crisis for these arrangements due to renewed inter-state rivalries, states' growing insecurities and arms racing problems. This is due to the fact that these arrangements are interconnected to strategic stability as many states' nuclear doctrines (discussed in the subsequent chapters) provide for nuclear retaliation to biological and chemical weapons attacks. Therefore, there is still need to reinforce these conventions thereby creating a new vision on how these treaties can be integrated into larger and increasingly integrated global security architecture. Since these treaties present a model for any future arrangement on nuclear disarmament, given their linkages with nuclear disarmament the proper and smooth functioning of these conventions becomes an important factor. In the nutshell, both the treaties are the true multilateral, non-discriminatory arrangements that ban use, proliferation and possession of these weapons. Any future crisis or demise of these treaties would affect nuclear disarmament endeavour. Thus these treaties need to be reinforced and strengthened in line with the future emerging security environment in order to take the global nuclear disarmament process forward.

Non-proliferation of conventional technologies

There is an important linkage between conventional and nuclear weapon technologies. For example, the conventional weapon asymmetries generate inter-states security problems that in turn increase their reliance on nuclear weapons to avert aggression. Threat of conventional asymmetries increases states' reliance on nuclear first-use doctrinal postures. This in turn creates stability-instability paradox[38] by decreasing nuclear thresholds and increasing fog of war between rival states.

On non-proliferation side, there are some treaties that not necessarily cover all but certain types of the conventional weapons/technologies. These treaties focus on regulating the transfer of arms and limiting employment of certain types of weapons to ensure strategic stability. Such instrument also bans certain types of weapons such as landmines and cluster weapons. For example, the Convention on Certain Conventional Weapons (CCWC) bans or restricts the use of specific types of weapons that are considered to cause unnecessary or unjustifiable suffering to combatants or to affect civilians indiscriminately. This is a very useful convention. Another treaty such as Conventional Armed Forces in Europe (CFE)[39] was negotiated during the final years of the Cold War, which is often referred to as the cornerstone of European security. This treaty eliminated the Soviet Union's overwhelming quantitative advantage in conventional weapons in Europe by setting up equal limits on weaponry that North Atlantic Treaty Organization and the Warsaw Pact could deploy between the Atlantic Ocean and the Ural Mountains. The treaty prevented either alliance from building forces for a blitzkrieg-type offensive, which could escalate to strategic levels. Although, the threat of such an offensive disappeared with the end of the Cold War and the disintegration of the Soviet Union, member states have repeatedly emphasized the long-term value of this treaty's weapons limits and inspection regime, which provided an unprecedented degree of transparency on military holdings.[40] Although CFE tried to promote regional balance but renewed great power competition has undermined CFE and Open Skies Treaty. The US lately withdrew from the 1992 Open Skies Treaty[41] despite domestic and global pressure to remain party to the accord.[42] Abrogation of Open Skies Treaty needs to be revived to promote disarmament.

The convention on the prohibition of the use, stockpiling, production and transfer of anti-personnel mines and on their destruction, commonly referred to as the Mine Ban Treaty. It is the most comprehensive international apparatus for eliminating landmines and deals with everything from mine use, production and trade, to victim assistance, mine clearance and stockpile destruction. States such as China, Egypt, India, Israel, Pakistan, Russia and the US[43] are not party to this treaty given their own security consideration against rival bordering states.

Convention on Cluster Munition is a legally binding international treaty that prohibits the use, production, stockpiling and transfer of cluster munitions and requires clearance of remnants and destruction of stocks. It requires states to provide assistance to survivors and their communities and builds on existing international human rights and humanitarian law.[44] Arms Trade Treaty (ATT)[45] is the first international legally binding agreement to establish standards for regulating the trade in conventional arms and preventing the illicit trade in weapons. The ATT process was backed by a coalition that brought together predominantly arms exporting states with states that primarily import arms or act as transit states. Support came from an uncommonly broad geographical range of countries. The process brought together the UN member states, non-governmental organizations (NGOs) and arms industry representatives. It benefited from the input of NGOs and government officials with experience from both the arms control field (where the focus is on banning or regulating particular categories of weapon) and the export controls field (where the focus is on standards for controlling international arms transfers).[46] The ATT had an opportunity for provision that could have incorporated the measures similar to that of BWC and CWC but they linked arms race to human security while the regional stability aspect was missing in it.

That said, the challenge is that many of the conventional technologies and lethal autonomous weapon systems are not covered in these protocols established against proliferation of conventional technologies. There are export control cartels such as WA and the MTCR. The WA has been established in order to contribute to the regional and international security and stability, by promoting transparency and greater responsibility in transfers of conventional arms and dual-use goods and technologies, thus preventing destabilizing accumulations. However, these are suppliers guided cartels that work on maximization of their own interests in disregard of states' growing capabilities that may lead to create insecurities of the other states. WA guidelines demonstrate that states will keep in mind the existing asymmetries in the region. However, it is a voluntary arrangement, therefore states do not follow these guidelines in true spirit. The MTCR aims[47] to limit the spread of ballistic missiles and other unmanned delivery systems that could be used for chemical, biological and nuclear attacks. This regime lacks legal legitimacy and is non-binding, introduced by the suppliers' states that follow their own criteria to maximize their interests. Thus, there exists enormous gap in the existing non-proliferation architecture to limit the production and transfer of conventional delivery system, UAVs, autonomous weapons and various other lethal conventional technologies.

Summing up, the above conventions are non-discriminatory and promote non-proliferation of certain types of conventional technologies. Some of the above protocols also promote stability through creating balance and building trust among states. Most of the treaties are promoting ban based on humanitarian ground such as land mine treaty and cluster munitions instead of maintaining balance or strategic stability. Similarly, CCWC is very effective arrangement that seeks to ban the use of certain conventional weapons whose effects are indiscriminate. Thus renewed mechanisms are needed to regulate/govern production and transfer of these weapons that in turn will help create new security environment and a clear road to nuclear disarmament (see subsequent chapters).

Arms control regime: Dent on multilateralism and disarmament

The US and Soviet Union negotiated different set of treaties during the peak of the Cold War that ensured bilateral trust and strategic stability but failed to craft a global arms control regime and a clear road to disarmament. Despite all the challenges confronted by the non-proliferation regime, the two superpowers built a precedent for bilateral arms control treaties that led to create stabilizing effects.[48] On the one hand, bilateral arms control negotiations led to minimize probability of war between the two superpowers while their persistent rivalries and influence on certain institutions led to challenge progress on nuclear disarmament. The two superpowers got past the brink of confrontation to enter into an era of détente. The US President Richard Nixon and Soviet leader Leonid Brezhnev pledged to permanently limit their countries' offensive nuclear arsenal. Thus, arms control mechanisms, a negotiating toolkit regulated some aspect of the US and Soviet military capabilities.

Since 1969, the US and Russia have been limiting their strategic nuclear arsenals through bilateral treaties. These arrangements began modestly with SALT I,[49] which only limited the number of ICBMs and SLBMs, leaving both nations to increase numbers of both bombers and warheads. SALT I also produced the ABM Treaty[50] in 1972, which banned nationwide strategic missile defences (the US withdrew from the ABM Treaty in 2002). Following the Cold War, START-I[51] (enacted in 1994), placed limitations on the numbers of deployed launchers and, for the first time, warheads. While, both START-II and III failed to materialize, the US and Russia negotiated the Strategic Offensive Reductions Treaty (SORT)[52] in 2002. SORT provided for a significant reduction of deployed strategic nuclear warheads in each arsenal to 1,700–2,200. However, SORT was often criticized for having a weak verification regime that relied on the START-I.

Initiated in 1987, bilaterally the most comprehensive arrangement, the INF Treaty, with far-reaching impact led to restraining both the US and Russia from developing nuclear and conventional ground-launched ballistic and cruise missiles with ranges between 500 and 5,500 km. Moreover, the two states agreed to pursue verifiable removal of 2,692 missiles deployed in Europe and the withdrawal of thousands of tactical nuclear weapons from forward-deployed locations. The treaty yielded result-oriented impact by building trust and strategic stability between the two states thereby benefitting and becoming a pillar of European security architecture[53] and setting normative trends globally in order to control horizontal and vertical proliferation. Nevertheless, the Trump administration has abrogated[54] the INF Treaty with Russia that was built over decades with consistent efforts and hard work by multiple US administrations. It has feared that the demise of the INF Treaty will fuel further arms race, driving other countries to acquire more weapons, thereby increasing the risks of accidental war, miscalculation and strategic instability.

The New START agreement which was signed in April 2010 and its subsequent entry into force in February 2011, limits the US and Russia to no more than 1,550 deployed nuclear warheads and 700 launchers by 2018.[55] Both the US and Russia met those limits on schedule, according to a February 2018 information exchange.[56] The renewal of the New START agreement for a period of five years by the Biden Administration gives hope that it will reverse trend of unravelling of painstaking negotiated arms control agreements starting from the demise of the ABM Treaty in 2002, the Open Skies Treaty 2020 and the INF Treaty. That said, both the US and Russia continue to pursue new types of weapons.[57] For example, at an annual address to the Russian parliament in the year 2018 and 2019, Russian President Vladimir Putin announced several new nuclear weapon delivery systems, including an intercontinental cruise missile,[58] while the US President Donald Trump's 2018 Nuclear Posture Review called for lower-yield warheads for SLBMs and submarine-launched cruise missiles.[59]

Question arises why the disarmament debate failed despite these positive efforts crafted by the two superpowers on reducing risks of war through arms control? The states rivalry kept disarmament at bay while the two superpowers remained focused on arms control in order to reduce risks of war.[60] These treaties were meant to secure the national security interests of the two states and were not a part of any global disarmament roadmap. The verification mechanisms were also limited to the two states with no multilateral involvement. Therefore, the treaties survival hinged on their relevance or otherwise for the national security interests of the two adversaries. Not unexpectedly then the US-Russia rivalries, emerging security environment, new technologies and rise of China led the US to abrogate the arms control treaties with Russia. These states' insecurities have converted into renewed security dilemma resulting into a spiral of action-reaction arms build-up across the region and globe thereby undermining the disarmament process.

Disarmament: The UN-led forums – who dominated whom?

The discussions on the UN platform and parallel disarmament negotiations among political groups have traversed since 1945. For example, within the UN-guided negotiations process, some formal political groups emerged who promoted disarmament through formal statement or submission of working papers.[61] The position was taken by the P-5 states representing the collective view of the NWS, NAM (representing over 100 non-western, developing NNWS seeking the immediate elimination of nuclear weapons by the P-5 countries), the New Agenda Coalition (repenting six prominent NNWS middle powers strongly in favour of nuclear disarmament), EU, the League of Arab States (each representing the common regional positions of their members).[62] However, despite many resolutions passed by the United Nations General Assembly (UNGA) on disarmament and multilateral negotiations (highlighted below) backed by the UN, through various forums, states failed to build consensus on nuclear disarmament. The gap widened between NWS (deterrent promoters) and NNWS (disarmament advocates) due to their divided opinions. The section below assesses how and why the global UN disarmament forums could not register any sizeable progress on disarmament?

The UN-led forums and disarmament failure

The very first resolution of the UNGA, in January 1946 underlined the challenges raised by the discovery of the atomic energy. The UN resolution established a commission to initiate a proposal for 'the elimination from national armament of atomic weapons and of all other major weapons adaptable to mass destruction.'[63] In 1952, the General Assembly passed a resolution 502 (VI) thereby creating the United Nations Disarmament Commission (UNDC) under the Security Council with a mandate to craft proposals for a treaty 'for the regulation, limitation and balanced reduction of all armed forces and all armaments, including the elimination of nuclear weapons.'[64] However, the commission assembled only occasionally after 1959. In the late 1950s, the US, Soviet Union, the United Kingdom and France initiated frozen disarmament talks that resulted into an agreement for a 7 September 1959 resolution of the UNDC, which facilitated the creation of the Ten-Nation Committee on Disarmament (TNCD) a new international negotiating forum.[65] Nevertheless, early efforts at the multilateral negotiations through a newly created TNCD made little progress without yielding any favourable dividends.[66]

During 1950s and 1960s, a range of more resolutions were adopted by the UNGA to discourage use of nuclear weapons, their further testing and horizontal proliferation.[67] The UN also offered a security framework that authorized the two superpowers for interface and discussions on the subject. However, later the UN apparatus made two superpowers' way out of the organization's framework for negotiations in order to preserve equal representation between the Eastern and the Western block. Thus, the new mechanism crafted by the two superpowers was the Eighteen Nation Disarmament Conference (ENDC) in 1961 which was sponsored by the UN.[68] Notably, the ENDC was assisted by the UN due to the fact that the negotiating body could respond to the recommendations made by the UNGA. The UNGA accepted the decision of the major powers to create the ENDC through its resolution 1722 (XVI) on 21 December 1961. The aim of the ENDC was to offer an international mechanism in order to deal with disarmament issues where the UN due to its mismanagement failed to deliver. The ENDC was proven to be a favourable platform than the UN in terms of its performance and securing membership of the non-aligned states.

The ENDC was co-chaired by the US and Soviet Union and both superpowers held discretionary political power to decide whether or not the ENDC would comply with the recommendations of the UNGA. By leaving the political initiative to the superpowers within the ENDC, the UN handed over to them a lot of power to sway the ENDC. This introduced a positive element into the negotiations as it led, at least, to the maintenance of a bilateral dialogue between the two superpowers within the body in 1960s. Arguably, the ENDC remained a successful and useful forum for multilateral negotiations. However, the challenge for the UN and the ENDC at this particular period was whether it would be possible for an indirect platform to achieve incremental peace through nuclear arms control arrangements in order to promote all-encompassing plans for General and Complete Disarmament (GCD).

Subsequently, the UNGA resolution 1664 (XVI) was passed that 'the countries not possessing nuclear weapons have a great interest and an important part to fulfil'[69] in banning nuclear tests and achieving nuclear disarmament. The UNGA resolution 1653 (XVI) went further noting that the targets of nuclear weapons would not just be 'enemies' but peoples of the world not involved in war, with deviation that would 'exceed even the scope of war and cause indiscriminate sufferings and destruction to mankind...contrary to the rules of international law and the law of humanity.'[70] Finally, the UNGA's resolution 1665 (XVI), unanimously adopted, called on NWS and NNWS to build cooperation on preventing further acquisition and spread of nuclear weapons.[71] That said, in the 1970s, the non-aligned group (disarmament supporters) emerged as the agenda-setting political driving force at the UN for the multilateral negotiating mechanism, which was renamed as the Conference of the Committee on Disarmament (CCD) in a distinct way from the ENDC. The ENCD (1962–1969) was succeeded by the CCD (1969–1978) until the CD was formed in 1979 (discussed below).

Notably, the CCD began work in 1969 and in addition to the name change, the General Assembly Resolution 2602 (XXIV) expanded its membership. For example, the CCD had a membership of 26 which later expanded to 31 in 1975[72] whereas the ENDC had 18 members only. Conspicuously, the CCD received instructions from and reported to the UNGA and like its two predecessors, this forum was also chaired and dominated by the US and Soviet Union. The CCD aimed at promoting efforts towards nuclear disarmament and conclusion of a CTBT in parallel to the quest for arms control arrangements. Notably, the revisions made in the UNGA's role led to make things worse because the real agenda-setting remained in the hands of the CCD and more particularly in the hands of the co-chairmen such as the US and Soviet Union instead of the UNGA. The negotiation process was contrary to the democratic norms. The non-aligned group wanted that the CCD should be capable of demonstrating completely its responsiveness to the UN. In fact, the non-aligned states found themselves uncomfortable in that sort of negotiating structure which is dominated by the two superpowers. For a better and a globally mainstreamed decision-making process on disarmament, the non-aligned states proceeded to revive the CCD with the very purpose of placing it politically under the UNGA's parameters in order to reorient them towards strengthening the role of the organization and confronting the 'big power tendency to manipulate or manage the World Organization according to their interests.'[73]

The direct consequence for the CCD was that it worked clumsily during this period, increasingly losing the focus on promoting efforts to achieve disarmament. The members of the CCD remained overwhelmed on the politics of the reforms of its structure and broadening the role of the UN. Indeed, the superpowers desired to retain control over their activities and the non-aligned aspired to eliminate such control. The reforms of the CCD, according to the non-aligned group's political expectations could lead to the uniting of all the diverse actors such as P-5 countries and non-aligned states in the disarmament process. They capitalized upon the potentialities of the polycentrism of those diverse actors to put up a powerful fight against the 'bilateral tendencies' which had eroded the role of the UN.

Special Session on Disarmament

The SSOD-I was backed and initiated by the non-aligned states to democratize international relations through the strengthening of the UN. The SSOD-I reflected a more comprehensive global disarmament forum and sought to address the imbalance of the NPT by laying down a roadmap of GCD and underscoring the principle of undiminished security for all states. It stipulates a stepwise approach to nuclear disarmament to ensure that at no step of the process one group of states gains advantage over others and undiminished security of all states is the fundamental goal.

The SSOD-I recognized limits with conventional asymmetries, role of new technologies, the significance international effective verification thereby complimenting regional and global approaches which was not in the provision of the NPT. More so, the SSOD-I laid down disarmament institutions and building blocks. The final document of the SSOD-1 provided explicitly for the right of all the states to participate in the negotiating process and reiterated their duty to do so. The outcome was a strong conviction that the institution-building of the UN disarmament machinery should be made in such a manner as to satisfy recognition of the fundamental democratic principle that 'all the states have a right to participate on an equal footing in the disarmament negotiations.'[74]

Furthermore, the non-aligned group was committed to expand the concept of security to encompass a broad political agenda that reflected the concerns of the majority of their members. Even before their emergence as the most powerful political grouping in terms of numerical strength in the UN, the concept of security, as it had been expressed in the Charter and developed in practice, had reflected predominantly military overtones. By the late 1970s, the presence of a different majority in the UN meant that the concept of economic security has been given more significance and this, in turn, meant that adherence to disarmament negotiations under the UN auspices would amount to an acceptance to negotiate nuclear disarmament on a North-South as well as an East-West basis. Thus far, the superpowers have not indicated a willingness to negotiate on such a basis. It is clear that the concept of security is understood differently when looked at from the East-West point of view rather than from that of the non-aligned.

Thus, the final document of the SSOD-1 explicitly accepts that disarmament and arms limitation, particularly in the nuclear field, facilitate the achievement of the New International Economic Order.[75] As it has been argued by the non-aligned states, the pursuit of disarmament is at the same time the pursuit of development by all nations. It is an integral part of the process of creating a new international order.[76] The outcome was the emergence of a new concept of security, a mixture of military and economic considerations, which resulted in legitimizing the active participation of all states on an equal basis in the negotiations, regardless of their military power. However, Cold War politics and superpowers' rivalries and security competition between states made progress difficult despite détente underpinned by the SALT I and SALT II, etc. It did, however, lead to reforms and modifications in the UN institution dealing with disarmament and identifying few milestones in this regard besides acknowledging the linkages between security, nuclear disarmament, other types of weapons and, technology and the elements of trust between them.

The Conference on Disarmament – repelling the debate

The CD was established in 1979 as the world's only permanent multilateral disarmament treaty negotiating body. Based in Geneva, the CD differs from the UNDC in that it is intended as a negotiation, rather than debating and advisory forum.[77] It also differs from the First Committee in that its focus is explicitly on the cessation of the nuclear arms race and nuclear disarmament as opposed to the First Committee's broader remit of international security and disarmament. Furthermore, in contrast to the NPT, the CD includes India, Pakistan, Israel and the Democratic People's Republic of Korea amongst its 65 members. Its negotiation remit thus spans not only the objective of nuclear disarmament amongst the P-5, but crucially also those non-NPT states parties who possess nuclear weapons and go unrecognized by the UNSC. The CD members are structured into four informal regional groups for the purposes of negotiations: the Western Group, the NAM Group of 21, the Eastern European Group and the Group of One (China).[78] The CD's consensus-based decision taking has often been blamed for the stalemate at this forum. Tariq Rauf commented, 'the CD, the sole multilateral arms control and disarmament forum, has been unable to agree on a negotiating mandate since 1996 when it completed the drafting of the Comprehensive Nuclear-Test-Ban Treaty. The reasons include differences in priorities of CD member states and also due to linkages between issues.'[79] Asif Durrani reflected, 'since NWS are not prepared to forego their arsenal, they have prevented the CD from agreeing on a roadmap for total elimination of nuclear weapons.'[80] However, it must also be acknowledged that CD has to its credit CWC and CTBT. The stalemate has therefore more to do with the security dynamics between the states outside the CD than the rules of procedures. Moreover, the General Assembly and its First Committee, where decision-making is by majority votes also failed to agree on concrete roadmap subsequent to the erosion of the consensus on SSOD-I which was undermined by the leading powers.

Negotiations on Fissile Material Cut-off Treaty (FMCT) in CD have been stalled even before start because of the divergence of views and scope. This again shows how the nuclear disarmament objective cannot be pursued in isolation from the real security consensus of the states in an environment where asymmetries both in the nuclear and conventional realms continue to threaten security of states. Another arrangement that can be extended to count the refrain regarding the CD consensus rule as a hurdle is the failure of the CTBT to entry into force despite its adaption. Security consensus/concerns of states can easily undermine adopted treaties. Commenting on working of the UN-led forums, Futter said, 'all these institutions will only be successful when the most powerful members want them to be.'[81]

Summing up, the disarmament forums failed to incorporate the spirit of the SSOD-I in their agenda. The forum beyond the SSOD-I lacked a holistic approach to nuclear disarmament. The above forums failed to maintain a parallel coordination with UN conflict resolution mechanisms. Despite strong linkages between conventional and non-conventional technologies, the states failed to introduce a multilateral mechanism to constrain conventional weapons. The existing conventional weapons-related efforts, treaties and conventions are not synthesized with CD's work on nuclear disarmament. Similarly, biological and chemical convention crisis linked to nuclear disarmament creates power rivalry which marred progress in the past has resurfaced in the present time. More so, the new technologies (discussed in the subsequent chapters) will increase states' reliance on nuclear weapons thereby undermining the efforts directed to nuclear disarmament.

Conclusion

The construct of nuclear non-proliferation, governing the WMDs is discriminatory and lacks rule-based criteria that has led to damage the credibility and stability of the regime thereby impacting the disarmament process. The NWS and NNWS are totally divided on total elimination of nuclear weapons. The parallel initiatives such as export control cartels or humanitarian efforts that aimed at strengthening the NPT norms and facilitate coordination among its member states failed to achieve their goals due to lack of coordination and democratization process. The P-5 states not only influenced all the review conferences but also made their implementation hard due to their national security considerations.

The states rivalry during the Cold War kept disarmament at bay while the two superpowers remained focused on arms control and non-proliferation in order to reduce risks of war. The verification mechanisms were also limited to the two states with no multilateral involvement. The disarmament debate lacks a multilateral treaty regime. These debates being promoted by the UN-led forums were influenced by the P-5 countries. Non-aligned states and humanitarian initiatives were powerful moves that led to create the SSOD–I which was later dominated and influenced by the power politics of P-5 states. The SSOD-I was the meaningful and comprehensive vision to promote the non-proliferation, arms control and disarmament on the basis of equality, justice and rules-based criteria. States' rivalries, P-5 countries influence and differences between the NWS and NNWS have marginalized the spirit of the SSOD-I. The forum beyond the SSOD-I lacked a holistic and inclusive approach to nuclear disarmament. All the treaties and conventions directed to promote non-proliferation of nuclear, biological and chemical weapons and nuclear disarmament lacked coordination with UN conflict resolution mechanisms. Despite strong linkages between conventional and non-conventional technologies, the states failed to introduce a multilateral mechanism to constrain conventional weapons. The existing conventional weapons-related treaties are not synthesized with CD's work on nuclear disarmament. Similarly, biological and chemical convention crisis linked to nuclear disarmament creates power rivalry which marred progress in the past has resurfaced in the present time.

The chapter proves that nuclear disarmament objective cannot be pursued in isolation from the real security consensus of the states in an environment where asymmetries both in the nuclear and conventional realms continue to threaten security of states. Security consensus of states can easily challenge the adopted treaties. The stalemate in the CD has therefore more to do with the security dynamics between the states outside the disarmament forums than the rules of procedures. For this, there is need to create a new security environment to build a new road to nuclear disarmament, which is discussed below.

Notes

1. Bernard Brodie (ed.), *The Absolute Weapon: Atomic Power and World Order* (New York: Harcourt, Brace, 1946).
2. See Thomas C. Shelling, *The Strategy of Conflict* (Cambridge, Massachusetts and London: Harvard University Press, 1980).
3. See Albert James Wohlstetter, 'The Delicate Balance of Terror,' *Foreign Affairs*, Vol. 37, No. 2 (1958), pp. 211–234: http://www.jstor.org/stable/20029345.
4. Patrick M. Morgan, *Deterrence Now* (Cambridge: Cambridge University Press, 2003), p. 8.
5. See Sverre Lodgaard, *Nuclear Disarmament and Non-Proliferation Towards a Nuclear-Weapons-Free World?* (London and New York: Routledge, 2011).

6. David Fischer, *History of the International Atomic Energy Agency: The First Forty Years* (Vienna: IAEA, 1997), p. 447.
7. See 'The Statute of the IAEA,' *International Atomic Energy Agency*: https://www.iaea.org/about/statute.
8. See 'Treaty on the Non-Proliferation of Nuclear Weapons (NPT),' *Office of the Disarmament Affairs, United Nations*: https://www.un.org/disarmament/wmd/nuclear/npt/.
9. Jan Priest, 'IAEA Safeguards and the NPT: Examining Interconnections,' *IAEA Bulletin*, Vol. 37, No. 1 (1995), p. 2: https://www.iaea.org/sites/default/files/publications/magazines/bulletin/bull37-1/37103480913.pdf.
10. Author's telephonic Interview with Andrew Futter, Professor of International Politics, *University of Leicester* (March 2021).
11. See 'JFK on Nuclear Weapons and Non-Proliferation,' *Carnegie Endowment for International Peace* (November 17, 2003): https://carnegieendowment.org/2003/11/17/jfk-on-nuclear-weapons-and-non-proliferation-pub-14652.
12. Nicholas L. Miller and Viping Narang, 'North Korea Defied the Theoretical Odds: What can we Learn from its Successful Nuclearization,' *Texas National Security Review*, Vol. 1, No. 2 (March, 2018), pp. 64–66: http://hdl.handle.net/2152/63943.
13. Joseph F. Pilat, 'The End of the NPT Regime?,' *International Affairs*, Vol. 83, No. 3 (2007), p. 473: https://doi.org/10.1111/j.1468-2346.2007.00632.x.
14. Hans M. Kristensen and Robert S. Norris, 'North Korean Nuclear Capabilities 2018,' *Bulletin of the Atomic Scientists*, Vol. 74, No. 1 (2018): pp. 41–46: https://doi.org/10.1080/00963402.2017.1413062.
15. See Ariane Tabatabai, *Nuclear Decision Making in Iran: Implications for US Non-proliferation Efforts* (New York: Columbia Center on Global Energy Policy, August 2020): https://www.energypolicy.columbia.edu/sites/default/files/file-uploads/IranNuclear_CGEP-Report_080520.pdf
16. Author's Interview with Andrew Futter.
17. Mark Hibbs, 'The Unspectacular Future of the IAEA Additional Protocol,' *Carnegie Endowment for International Peace* (April 26, 2012): http://carnegieendowment.org/2012/04/26/unspectacular-future-of-iaea-additional-protocol-pub-47964.
18. Adrian Levy, 'India is Building a Top-Secret Nuclear City to Produce Thermonuclear Weapons Experts Say,' *Foreign Policy* (December 16, 2015): https://foreignpolicy.com/2015/12/16/india_nuclear_city_top_secret_china_pakistan_barc/
19. Mark Hibbs, 'Eyes on the Prize: India's Pursuit of Membership in the Nuclear Suppliers Group,' *The Nonproliferation Review*, Vol. 24, No. 3–4 (2017), pp. 275–296: https://doi.org/10.1080/10736700.2018.1436253.
20. Tariq Rauf and Rebecca Johnson, 'After the NPT's Indefinite Extension: The future of Nonproliferation Regime,' *Nonproliferation Review*, Vol. 3, No. 1 (Fall 1995), p. 34: https://doi.org/10.1080/10736709508436604.
21. David Krieger, 'Participation in the 1995 NPT Review and Extension Conference,' *Nuclear Age Peace Foundation* (April 9, 2019): https://www.wagingpeace.org/participation-in-the-1995-npt-review-and-extension-conference/.
22. Ibid.

23. Ibid.
24. Jan Prawitz and James F. Leonard, *A Zone Free of Weapons of Mass Destruction in the Middle East* (New York and Geneva: United Nations Publication, 1996), p. 60: https://unidir.org/sites/default/files/publication/pdfs/a-zone-free-of-weapons-of-mass-destruction-in-the-middle-east-134.pdf.
25. Jayantha Dhanapala and Randy Rydell, 'Multilateral Diplomacy and the NPT: An Insider's Account,' in Jayantha Dhanapala and Tariq Rauf (ed.), *Reflections on the Treaty on the Non-Proliferation of Nuclear Weapons: Review Conferences and the Future of the NPT* (Stockholm International Peace Research Institute, 2016), p. 109.
26. Ibid., p. 101.
27. See 'Remarks by President Barack Obama in Prague as Delivered,' (April 5, 2009): https://obamawhitehouse.archives.gov/the-press-office/remarks-president-barack-obama-prague-delivered.
28. See 'Final Document Review Conference of the Parties to the Treaty on the Non-Proliferation of Nuclear Weapons,' *United Nations* (New York, 2010): https://www.un.org/ga/search/view_doc.asp?symbol=NPT/CONF.2010/50%20(VOL.I).
29. Tariq Rauf, 'Assessing the 2015 NPT Review Conference,' in Jayantha Dhanapala and Tariq Rauf (ed.), *Reflections on the Treaty on the Non-Proliferation of Nuclear Weapons: Review Conferences and the Future of the NPT* (Stockholm International Peace Research Institute, 2016), p. 208.
30. Richard Guthrie, John Hart, and Farida Kahlau, 'Chemical and Biological Warfare Developments and Arms Control', in SIPRI Yearbook 2006: Armaments, Disarmament and International Security (Stockholm International Peace Research Institute, 2006), pp. 707–730.
31. Ibid.
32. Chris Reynolds. 'Global Health Security and Weapons of Mass Destruction Chapter,' in *Global Health Security: Recognizing Vulnerabilities, Creating Opportunities* (Switzerland: Springer, 2020), pp. 187–207.
33. Eitan Barak, 'Getting the Middle East Holdouts to Join the CWC,' *Bulletin of the Atomic Scientists* (January/ February 2010), pp. 57-61: https://doi.org/10.2968%2F066001008.
34. Ibid.
35. Ibid.
36. Ibid.
37. Oliver Meier and Ralf Trapp, 'Playing Politics with Chemical Weapons? The UK's Initiative on Chemical Weapons Accountability,' *The Bulletin of the Atomic Scientist* (June 20, 2018): https://thebulletin.org/2018/06/playing-politics-with-chemical-weapons-the-uks-initiative-on-chemical-weapons-accountability/.
38. Michael Krepon, 'The Stability-Instability Paradox in South Asia,' *Stimson Centre* (January 1, 2005): https://www.stimson.org/2005/stability-instability-paradox-south-asia/.
39. Anne Witkowsky, Sherman Garnett and Jeff McCausland, 'Salvaging the Conventional Armed Forces in Europe Treaty Regime: Options for Washington,' *Brooking Arms Control Series*, Paper 2 (March 2010), pp. 1–8.

40. Daryl Kimball and Kingston Reif, 'The Conventional Armed Forces in Europe (CFE) Treaty and the Adapted CFE Treaty at a Glance,' *Arms Control Association* (August, 2017): https://www.armscontrol.org/factsheet/cfe.
41. Open Skies Treaty permitted countries to fly unarmed aircraft with cameras and other sensors over the territory of the Treaty's other 34 Members' States.
42. Kingston Reif and Shannon Bugos, 'U.S. Completes Open Skies Treaty Withdrawal,' *Arms Control Association* (December 2020): https://www.armscontrol.org/act/2020-12/news/us-completes-open-skies-treaty-withdrawal.
43. Daryl Kimball, 'The Ottawa Convention at a Glance,' *Arms Control Association* (August, 2018): https://www.armscontrol.org/factsheets/ottawa.
44. Daryl Kimball, 'Cluster Munitions at a Glance,' *Arms Control Association* (December, 2017): https://www.armscontrol.org/factsheets/clusterataglance.
45. Daryl G. Kimball, 'The Arms Trade Treaty at a Glance,' *Arms Control Association* (August, 2017): https://www.armscontrol.org/factsheets/arms_trade_treaty.
46. Sibylle Bauer, Paul Beijer and Mark Bromley, 'The Arms Trade Treaty: Challenges for the First Conference of States Parties,' *SIPRI Insight on Peace and Security*, No. 2014/2 (September, 2014), p. 1: https://www.sipri.org/sites/default/files/files/insight/SIPRIInsight1402.pdf.
47. Kelsey Davenport, 'The Missile Technology Control Regime at a Glance', *Arms Control Association* (December 2004): https://www.armscontrol.org/factsheets/mtcr.
48. Joseph S. Nye Jr., 'Arms control after the Cold War,' *Foreign Affairs*, Vol. 68, No. 5 (Winter 1989), pp. 45–46: https://doi.org/10.2307/20044199.
49. Steve Smith, 'US-Soviet Strategic Nuclear Arms Control: From SALT to START to Stop,' *Arms Control,* Vol. 5, No. 3 (1984), pp. 51–53: https://doi.org/10.1080/01440388408403803.
50. Ibid., pp. 52–53.
51. Amy F. Woolf, *Strategic Arms Control after START: Issues and Options* (Congressional Research Service: March 4, 2010), p. 1.
52. Nikolai Sokov, 'The Russian Nuclear Arms Control Agenda after SORT,' *Arms Control Today* Vol. 33, No. 3 (April, 2003), p. 7: https://search.proquest.com/openview/dfe586e4e98265332c31937eb9e9800a/1?pq-origsite=gscholar&cbl=37049.
53. Alexander Lanoszka, 'The INF Treaty: Pulling Out in Time,' *Strategic Studies Quarterly,* Vol. 13, No. 2 (2019), pp. 49-51: https://www.jstor.org/stable/26639673.
54. Ibid., p. 48.
55. Amy F. Woolf, *The New START Treaty: Central Limits and Key Provisions* (Congressional Research Service: August 27, 2014), pp. 1–3.
56. Steven Pifer, 'Unattainable Conditions for New START Extension?,' *Brookings* (July 1, 2020): https://www.brookings.edu/blog/order-from-chaos/2020/07/01/unattainable-conditions-for-new-start-extension/.
57. Michael T. Klare, 'An 'Arm Race in Speed': Hypersonic Weapons and the Changing Calculus of Battle,' *Arms Control Today*, Vol. 49, No. 5 (2019), p. 6: https://www.jstor.org/stable/26755134.

58. Anton Troianovski, 'Putin Claims Russia is Developing Nuclear Arms Capable of Avoiding Missile Defenses, *The Washington Post*, (March 1, 2018): https://www.washingtonpost.com/world/europe/putin-claims-russia-has-nuclear-arsenal-capable-of-avoiding-missile-defenses/2018/03/01/d2dcf522-1d3b-11e8-b2d9-08e748f892c0_story.html.
59. Olga Oliker, 'US and Russian Nuclear Strategies Lowering Thresholds, Internationally and Otherwise,' in Caroline Dorminey and Eric Gormez (ed.), *America's Nuclear Crossroads a Forward-looking anthology* (CATO Institute: Washington, 2019), p. 37.
60. Author's Interview with Kamran Akhtar, D.G. Arms Control and Disarmament, Ministry of Foreign Affairs, Pakistan (December 2020).
61. See 'Conference on Disarmament,' *Nuclear Threat Initiative* (June 26, 2020): https://www.nti.org/learn/treaties-and-regimes/conference-on-disarmament/.
62. Megan Dee, 'Group Dynamics and Interplay in UN Disarmament Forum: In Search of Consensus,' *The Hague Journal of Diplomacy*, Vol. 12, No. 2–3 (2017), pp. 161–162: https://doi.org/10.1163/1871191X-12341364.
63. See 'Establishment of a Commission to Deal with the Problems Raised by the Discovery of Atomic Energy,' *United Nations General Assembly*:https://www.un.org/ga/search/view_doc.asp?symbol=A/RES/1(I).
64. See 'United Nations Disarmament Commission,' *Office for Disarmament Affairs, United Nations:* https://www.un.org/disarmament/institutions/disarmament-commission/.
65. Coit D. Blacker and Gloria Duffy, *International Arms Control: Issues and Agreements* (Stanford: Stanford University Press, 1984), p. 109.
66. Joseph L. Nogee, 'Propaganda and Negotiations: The Case of the Ten-Nation Disarmament Committee,' *Journal of Conflict Resolution*, Vol. 7, No. 3 (September 1, 1963), pp. 510–521: https://doi.org/10.1177/002200276300700334.
67. Jane Boulden, Ramesh Thakur and Thomas G. Weiss, 'The United Nations and the Nuclear Orders: Contexts, Foundations, Actors, Tools and Future Prospects,' in Jane Boulden, Ramesh Thakur and Thomas G. Weiss (ed.), *The United Nations and Nuclear Orders* (Tokyo, New York and Paris: United Nations University Press, 2009), p. 4.
68. Albert Legault and Michel Fortmann, *A Diplomacy of Hope Canada and Disarmament 1945-1988* (London: Mc-Gill Queen's University Press, 1992), p. 197.
69. See 'Declaration on the Prohibition of the Use of Nuclear and Thermonuclear Weapons,' *United Nations General Assembly* (24 November 1961): https://www.refworld.org/docid/528c8d1b4.html.
70. Ibid.
71. Ibid.
72. Manouchehr Fartash, 'The Disarmament Club's at Work,' *Bulletin of the Atomic Scientists*, Vol. 33, No. 1 (1977), p. 57: https://doi.org/10.1080/00963402.1977.11458324.
73. Odette Jankowitsch and Karl P. Sauvant, *The Third World without Superpowers: The Collected Documents of the Non-Aligned Countries Vol. I* (New York: Oceania Publications, 1978), pp. 203 & 501.

74. Randy J. Rydel, 'Bringing Democracy to Disarmament A Historical Perspective on the Special Sessions of the General Assembly Devoted to Disarmament,' *UNODA Occasional Paper,* No. 29 (New York: United Nations, 2016), pp. 11–20.
75. Peter Jones and Demetris Bourantonis, 'The United Nations and Nuclear Disarmament: A Case Study in Failure', *Current Research on Peace and Violence*, Vol. 13, No. 1 (1990), pp. 7–15: https://www.jstor.org/stable/40725140.
76. Ibid.
77. Jozef Goldbalt, 'The Conference on Disarmament at the Crossroads: To Revitalize or Dissolve?,' *The Nonproliferation Review* Vol. 7, No. 2 (2000), p. 104:https://doi.org/10.1080/10736700008436813.
78. See 'Geneva-Based Conventions and Treatise,' *Office for Disarmament Affairs, United Nations*: https://www.ungeneva.org/en/topics/disarmament.
79. Author's interview with Tariq Rauf, currently is a Vienna-based expert on nuclear governance matters, and Director of Atomic Reporters, March 11, 2021.
80. Author's interview with Asif Durrani, who has served in various Missions of Pakistan abroad including New Delhi, Tehran, New York, Kabul and London.
81. Author's interview with Andrew Futter.

2 Competing approaches
Identifying the gaps

Introduction

The history of nuclear weapons cannot be separated from the debates of disarmament which generally emphasize the idea of total elimination of nuclear weapons. Besides state-centric approaches, the global aspiration for a nuclear disarmament has manifested itself in various unilateral, bilateral and multilateral initiatives for a world free of nuclear weapons.

In the world of power politics structured on the uncompromising values of national interests, the states equipped with nuclear weapons rarely endorse the idea of disarmament out of their hypothetical domains. The vision for creating a world free of nuclear weapons matters less for the leaders of great power due to their competing geostrategic interests which are mainly inherited in the concept of *Realpolitik*. As evident from the decades long history of nuclear politics, marked by the US-Soviet rivalry during the Cold War, the idea of *Realpolitik* and its undeniable relevance to the varying patterns of world politics has hindered the progress of disarmament in the international system.

For the five permanent members of the United Nations Security Council, the nuclear NPT constituted the cornerstone for the global non-proliferation and disarmament. While the NPT succeeded in large part in limiting the number of nuclear possessor states, it left much to be desired in terms of achieving the goal of elimination of nuclear weapons or preventing their vertical proliferation. The Article VI of the NPT placed a general obligation on NWS to 'pursue negotiations in good faith on effective measures relating to cessation of the nuclear arms race at an early date and to nuclear disarmament, and on a treaty on general and complete disarmament under strict and effective international control.'[1] However, it stopped short of providing a concrete roadmap to this end or assigning any role to the IAEA in that regard.

DOI: 10.4324/9781003131205-2

In the face of frustrating progress on nuclear disarmament between the five NWS, various initiatives emerged on nuclear disarmament parallel to the regular inter-governmental interactions. These initiatives were guided by humanitarian or normative considerations in contrast with the security-centric approaches of the NWS. To understand the role of non-governmental approaches to disarmament originating from various directions, it is essential to maintain a chronological survey of disarmament efforts established on normative or humanitarian standards in order to build an assessment as to why these initiatives failed to convince the states to achieve nuclear disarmament.[2] This chapter endeavours to understand the role of disarmament initiatives which were structured beyond the framework of the P-5 dominated nuclear disarmament discourse and their effectiveness or ineffectiveness to convince the NWS on disarmament endeavour.

Humanitarian/normative initiatives

The humanitarian approaches for promoting the agenda of a nuclear-free world is fundamentally inherited in the notion of human security contrary to the state-centred view of national security. The goal of denuclearizing the whole world is an attempt of international community for eliminating or reducing the military capabilities which can cause an unimaginable catastrophe against humanity. Nuclear disarmament initiatives grounded in humanitarian concerns for preventing a catastrophic and deadly nuclear war between nations emerged from different corners of the world. For the purpose of dynamic humanitarian actions against the overwhelming role of nuclear weapons in the world politics, the proponents of peace and humanity in the world have acquired the legality from the humanistic values of international law. The groups advocating the vision of denuclearization across the globe emerged in non-governmental circles across the globe. The transcending humanistic attributes of different societies from across the world constituted the driving force for the various humanitarian initiatives at the international level right after the advent of nuclear weapons.

Since the US bombings of Hiroshima and Nagasaki, the catastrophic effects of nuclear weapons motivated ordinary citizens to push their leaders to pursue arms control and disarmament measures to reduce the threat of nuclear weapons use.[3] The radioactive fallout from nuclear weapons testing was drawn to public attention in 1954 when a hydrogen bomb test in the Pacific contaminated the crew of the Japanese fishing boat Lucky Dragon.[4] One of the fishermen died in Japan seven months later, which in turn generated widespread concerns around the world and 'provided a decisive impetus for the emergence of the anti-nuclear weapons movement in many countries.'[5] Peace movements emerged in Japan and in 1954 they converged to form a unified Japanese Council against Atomic and Hydrogen Bombs. Japanese opposition to the Pacific nuclear weapons tests was prevalent, and an estimated 35 million signatures were collected on petitions calling for bans on nuclear weapons.[6] Significantly, in the wake of initiation of nuclear arms racing, Bertrand Russell[7] conceived the idea that the scientists should be aware of the catastrophic consequences of their scientific works that led to release of Russell-Einstein Manifesto in 1955.[8] The Pugwash Conferences on Science and World Affairs was founded in 1957 by Joseph Rotblat and Bertrand Russell[9] focusing on issues like the threat of nuclear war, arms limitations and eventually towards the general and complete disarmament. The Pugwush played meaningful role during the Cold War era in a sense that it provided a useful platform for communication between the rival states specifically at a time when formal channels of negotiations were suspended due to increasing tensions. The organizational endeavours served as a significant input to official negotiations on numerous international treaties such as Partial Test Ban Treaty, NPT, Strategic Arms Limitation Treaty I and Biological Weapons Convention.[10] Rotblat and the Pugwash Conference were honoured with the Nobel Peace Prize in 1995 for their outstanding efforts on nuclear disarmament.[11]

The global concern on banning of nuclear weapons appeared from the United Kingdom with the publication of an article 'British and the Nuclear Bombs,'[12] which became a prominent expression of a nationwide campaign in the United Kingdom for unilaterally declaring its support for disarmament in 1957 which later formulated a Campaign for Nuclear Disarmament (CND),[13] recognized as the largest anti-nuclear bomb movements in the West.[14] This campaign gradually started calling for global ban on nuclear weapons.[15] The British opinions on the formulation of a nuclear-free international society inspired nuclear disarmament activism in other regions of the world. The European continent witnessed a major social movement promoting the idea of denuclearization across Europe. It was mainly introduced and promoted by Bertrand Russell Peace Foundation, established in 1963,[16] created to carry forward the ideas of peace, human rights and social justice[17] under the umbrella of a campaign for European Nuclear Disarmament (END). The END became a wide movement of Europe for creating a nuclear-free Europe. The collaboration between the CND and END issued an 'Appeal for European Disarmament' in 1980.[18]

The mutual efforts for the advancement of nuclear disarmament campaign in the world further glorified the idea of peace and development linked to the general concept of denuclearization. These movements collectively generated widespread awareness on humanitarian aspect of nuclear weapons and significance of total elimination of these weapons.

Eventually, independent voices for protecting the world from the dangers of nuclear weapons emerged from different corners of the world. In 1959, the Nobel Peace Prize was awarded to Philip J. Noel-Baker for his extensive intellectual contribution in the field of disarmament. Noel-Baker, a famous diplomat and a renowned academician, was an active proponent of denuclearization who supported the multilateral format of disarmament in 1950s.[19] Along with Noel-Baker, another British politician, Fenner Brockway, founded the World Disarmament Campaign in 1979 which focused an international disarmament plan structured on a multilateral consensus instead of unilateral and bilateral formats of denuclearization in the nuclear and non-nuclear domains.[20] Another peace educator and a non-violence campaigner from New Zealand, Alyn Ware, started supporting the global agenda of banning nuclear weapons. Ware was instrumental in concluding a plan for No Nukes, No War which became a famous campaign Abolition 2000: Global Network to Eliminate Nuclear Weapons in 1995.[21] Later on, it transformed into a global coalition of more than 2,000 organizations and also brought on board different governments willing to conclude a global treaty for the elimination of nuclear weapons.[22] In that sense these movements were instrumental in convincing NNWS on their agenda.

In midst of Cold War period, witnessing an extreme divide between the nuclear 'Haves' and 'Have-nots,'[23] the European religious circles also proved to be vocal anti-nuclear advocates involving their cross-cultural and cross-border associations. A Dutch peace movement emerged in the form of Interchurch Peace Council (IKV) in 1966[24] aimed against the emerging arms race in the world by calling it a *No to Use* equally to a *No to Possession* based on a global two-sided disarmament agenda during the peak of Cold War competition.[25] These voices were widespread at the grassroots level, thus transcending effects globally.

Gradually, the inspiration for peace and humanity was joined by other civil society groups. In 1980, the International Physicians for the Prevention of Nuclear War (IPPNW)[26] was established, mainly consisting of many medical groups of doctors, health workers and students. The IPPNW was comprised of physicians from both East and

West including members from the US and Soviet Union. The association worked for both complete abolition of nuclear weapons and cautious interim measures developed to slow down arms racing or create the trust necessary for its cessation.[27] The American-based IPPNW received Nobel Peace Prize in 1985.[28]

In 1982, Nuclear Age Peace Foundation (NAPF) was created with the mission of supporting the notion of a peaceful world order through educating and enlightening the international society about the vision of a denuclearized international system.[29] The NAPF later compelled its creators to persuade the state governments on the agenda of nuclear zero in 2014 with the consultation of the Republic of the Marshall Islands (RMI). The RMI filed a lawsuit against the nine NWS in the International Court of Justice[30] for making their governments accountable for not adhering to the global disarmament agenda. While keeping the nine nuclear weapons states (five de jure, three de facto and North Korea) in the same category, the RMI demanded accountability of signatories and non-signatories to the NPT for the lack of substantial progress in their obligation of disarmament.[31] So, the objective, the world free of nuclear weapons gradually became a momentous agenda with the further addition of the ICAN. The ICAN was a transnational civil society alliance which came into being in 2007 for drawing the attention of political authorities for denouncing the role of nuclear weapon in the world.[32] The Australia-based civil society coalition popularized its agenda around the globe, and was awarded with the Nobel Peace Prize in 2017 on the completion of a decade.[33] The founding members of the ICAN were instrumental in concluding the Ottawa Treaty (commonly known as Mine Ban Treaty).[34] However, the far-reaching outcome of the ICAN efforts was its persuasion of the UN members on the adoption of the UN Treaty on the Prohibition of Nuclear Weapons.

The global movement which emerged in the world for promoting the ideas of denuclearization in the last phase of the Cold War enlightened the notion of disarmament across the world. The purpose of these movements was to rid the whole humanity from the shadows of war by sensitizing the leaders of the great powers towards the consequences of nuclear war.[35] It was a societal effort where the participating public opinion-makers focused the idea of denouncing the existence of nuclear arms from the world politics in 1982.[36] The various initiatives, which cut across regions and were founded on common conception of a world free of nuclear weapons initiated a symbolic struggle for the advancement of nuclear disarmament in the world politics. In this regard, the biggest alliance for the promotion of nuclear disarmament appeared in the form of The Ribbon International on the basis of the Justine Merritt's ideas in 1982.[37] The Ribbon International gradually became a prime UN non-governmental initiative, and an active global forum for arranging various peace protests in different American states. In parallel, the other anti-nuclear activists have also designed many forums to raise their slogan of denuclearization across the US such as the Alliance for Nuclear Accountability (ANA) which was formed in 1987. The ANA is active in sensitizing the US federal government about the negative impacts of nuclear weapons facilities with the help of an alliance of various local, regional and national organizations.[38] The American history has seen a massive call for disarmament in 1986 when the protesters from different states were united for advancing the agenda of total elimination of nuclear weapons.[39] Like Washington, the other capitals of the world also witnessed social movements and independent voices demanding the total elimination of nuclear weapons.

A global network of around 800 parliamentarians from more than 80 countries has formed a cross-national and cross-cultural alliance calling for nuclear non-proliferation and disarmament. The Parliamentarians for Nuclear Non-Proliferation and Disarmament provide different positions on the issues of disarmament and nuclear proliferation.[40] The contemporary norm of humanitarian disarmament appeared in the mainstream humanitarian debates in the international system in 1990s. The debate on the nuclear disarmament reached every region, and the states from different parts of the world started considering the role of inter-governmental and non-governmental organizations working with or without the UN auspices as an important part of international system.[41] The campaign for multilateral disarmament for creation of an international society free from nuclear weapons sensitized the international community and led to the observation by the UN observing an annual day as of the International Day for the Total Elimination of Nuclear Weapons on September 26 of every year. The UN General Assembly Resolution 68/72 of December 2013 designated this annual day as a reminder to Member States on keeping nuclear disarmament in their national priorities.[42] In line with the evolving debate on nuclear weapons-free world, international organizations working in different humanitarian fields also started raising their voices for the universal disarmament. The International Committee of Red Cross showed its commitment for the total elimination of nuclear weapons and universal disarmament. International Federation of Red Cross and Red Crescent Societies and the International Red Cross and Red Crescent Movement started supporting the greater agenda of civil society envisioning an international system beyond the nuclear shades.[43] Several other organizations such as the Amnesty International, Human Rights Watch and Oxfam have also espoused the cause on the banning of nuclear weapons. The aforementioned initiatives have finally merged into an international movement that has made a significant contribution in generating global awareness and reaching out to the UN forums highlighting the need for total elimination of these catastrophic weapons.

The alliance of civil society and governments

Since the advent of nuclear weapons, there is a growing impatience within the international community to bring this threat to humanity to an end once and for all. This impatience arises from the lack of progress towards abolition, despite legally binding nuclear disarmament obligations, millions of citizens having campaigned for disarmament over the years and the attendant rhetoric of governments about creating a world free of nuclear weapons.[44] Much like the frustration of the civil society, many NNWS have been feeling that the NWS have felt to keep their side of the bargain enshrined in the NPT by dragging their feet on nuclear disarmament. This shared frustration has led certain governments to join hands with the civil society to promote progress towards a world free of nuclear weapons. Some of the initiatives include the New Agenda Coalition (NAC).[45] In June 1998, Foreign Ministers from Brazil, Egypt, Ireland, Mexico, New Zealand, South Africa, Slovenia and Sweden (the latter two eventually withdrawing), issued a statement calling for a new nuclear disarmament agenda, 'Toward a Nuclear-Weapons-Free World: Time for a New Agenda.'[46] The basic objective of the initiative was to give a thrust to political momentum toward nuclear disarmament which was facing stagnation in progress.[47] The NAC played an instrumental role in convincing the NWS to agree to the thirteen practical steps towards nuclear disarmament in the final document of the 2000 NPT Review Conference.[48]

Around the same time, the Middle Powers Initiative (MPI) was established which brought seven international non-governmental organizations (INGOs)[49] under one umbrella in order to build bridges between governments' (NNWS) efforts to reduce and eliminate worldwide nuclear weapons arsenals. The forum assisted the 'middle powers countries' which are considered to be significant economically as well as politically in the international system and also has renounced the arms racing, to work with the NWS for the purpose of reduction and elimination of nuclear weapons. In the wake of the 2005 NPT

Review Conference failure, the MPI launched the 'Article VI Forum' in October 2005 to examine the legal, technical, and political requirements to fulfil non-proliferation and disarmament commitments for a nuclear weapon-free world.[50]

Adding to this effort has been the work of several independent international commissions which played an important role by providing expert recommendations in the form of nuclear disarmament action plans. These commissions include the 1996 Canberra Commission on the Elimination of Nuclear Weapons sponsored by the Australian Government,[51] the 1998 Tokyo Forum for Nuclear Non-proliferation and Disarmament sponsored by the Japanese government,[52] and the Weapons of Mass Destruction Commission.[53] The WMD Commission issued a report that concluded 'the nuclear-weapon states no longer seem to take their commitment to nuclear disarmament seriously-even though this was an essential part of the NPT bargain, both at the treaty's birth in 1968 and when it was extended indefinitely in 1995.'[54] The report offered several recommendations for multilateral cooperative actions to counter this trend, including a call to adhere to disarmament obligations, ratify the CTBT and FMCT, and change nuclear postures.

Effectiveness of this coalition was that the two highly significant treaties were achieved through humanitarian processes led by cross-regional groups of enlightened Governments in partnership with transnational civil society exerting pressure and providing information and strategies. By reframing prohibition treaty imperatives in humanitarian terms rather than in terms of control and non-proliferation, it became possible to ban anti-personnel landmines and cluster munitions through treaties that entered into force in 1999 and 2010, respectively.[55] Meanwhile negotiations under the United Nations auspices developed the 2001 Program of Action on Small Arms and the 2013 ATT.

An initiative, undertaken by four former high-ranking US officials such as George Shultz, William Perry, Henry Kissinger and Sam Nunn, created significant momentum for a world free of nuclear weapons.[56] The four statesmen originally published their proposals, 'A World Free of Nuclear Weapons'[57] followed a year later by another op-ed, 'Toward a Nuclear Weapon Free World.'[58] This initiative came at a critical juncture, with the international community facing new and ongoing nuclear threats, when no new significant arms control reductions between the US and Russia was being pursued. The four statesmen called for the US leadership and global cooperation on non-proliferation.

Meanwhile the P-5 process initiated by the United Kingdom in 2008 with an objective to implement the disarmament commitments under the umbrella of the NPT. The forum was developed to initiate multilateral confidence building measures; relating to their nuclear forces, within the NWS to support other bilateral and multilateral nuclear initiatives. In fact, the supporters of the P-5 process anticipated that cooperation among NWS could gradually create sustainable impetus toward nuclear disarmament.[59]

In 2008, Japan and Australia established the International Commission on Nuclear Non-Proliferation and Disarmament to reinvigorate international non-proliferation and disarmament efforts and to help shape a consensus at the then-upcoming 2010 NPT Review Conference. Japan and Australia joined together again in September 2010 to create the Non-proliferation and Disarmament Initiative (NPDI). The group consisted of twelve countries including Australia, Canada, Chile, Germany, Japan, Mexico, the Netherlands, Nigeria, the Philippines, Poland, Turkey and the United Arab Emirates[60] that aimed to facilitate the implementation of the measures from the consensus document of the 2010 NPT Review Conference.[61] In April 2014, the NPDI adopted the 'Hiroshima Declaration' that contained concrete proposals for both disarmament and non-proliferation, including calls to negotiate the FMCT, increase nuclear safety and safeguards, encourage the entry into force of the CTBT, and increase transparency in disarmament reporting.[62] However, as the NPDI consists mainly of the US allies protected by the US extended nuclear deterrence, its disarmament approach is often considered more moderate than the ones of the NAC or Non-Aligned Movement (NAM) that call for delegitimizing nuclear weapons.

The increasing attention on the humanitarian impact of nuclear weapons led the adoption by the 2010 NPT Review Conference of the final document expressing concern about the humanitarian consequences of any use of nuclear weapons.[63] The coalition of state parties and civil society groups has continued to push this issue, resulting in three international conferences on the humanitarian impact of nuclear weapons in Oslo, Nayarit and Vienna, where there have been discussions about negotiating a prohibition against nuclear weapons.[64] The third conference in Vienna produced the Humanitarian Pledge (formerly the Austrian Pledge), which 127 countries have supported.[65] The joint statement emphasized that nuclear weapons should never be used again 'under any circumstances.'[66]

Some other significant initiatives that are relevant to achieving a goal of nuclear-free world specifically on part of states (including

NWS, NNWS, the UN and civil society) include the step-by-step approach to nuclear disarmament advanced by the Group of Non-Aligned States (110 plus NAM States in 2010, 2015 and 2019); the humanitarian initiative on the impact of nuclear weapons advanced in 2013 (Norway), 2014 (Mexico and Austria), 2015 (by Austria and 158 other countries);[67] the US-led creating the environment for near disarmament[68] and the Stockholm Initiative (2018) on stepping stones to nuclear disarmament advanced by Sweden and 15 other countries.[69]

The significant and tireless efforts by the civil society, in partnerships with several governments, eventually led to the adoption of the TPNW in July 2017. While this marked a significant normative development, none of the nuclear possessor states participated in the negotiations of the TPNW or has signed onto it. Even from among those who participated in the negotiations, the TPNW was adopted by a recorded vote of 122 in favour to one against (the Netherlands), with one abstention (Singapore).[70]

Proponents of the TPNW believe that it can strengthen norms against nuclear weapons and stigmatize such weapons. Opponents, including nuclear possessing states and states under extended nuclear deterrence, boycotted the negotiations (with the exception of the Netherlands). NWS have been sharply critical of the treaty process; France, the United Kingdom and the US released a joint statement asserting that the treaty deepens the divide between NWS and NNWS, and that they do not 'intend to sign, ratify or ever become party to it.'[71] Russian federation viewed the TPNW to be parting its way from NPT and opposed it by claiming that 'This initiative makes no contribution to the advancement towards the noble goal declared. Quite on the contrary it threatens the very existence and efficiency of our fundamental Non-proliferation treaty.'[72]

Durrani said, 'the proponents of TPNW have a moral and a legitimate case which unfortunately is at odds with realpolitik. Its efficacy is weak, to say the least. Nuclear weapons are not anti-personnel mines or cluster munitions or small arms which are visible and whose impact is felt and seen on television screens. Impacts of nuclear weapons are known but difficult to be hardwired into global public psyche.'[73] On TPNW, Futter said, 'it's problematic having a treaty [on disarmament] that does not include NWS.' Futter considers the TPNW a significant move but he doesn't think if it is going to yield any tangible impact anytime soon.

However, the majority of the international community welcomed the adoption of the treaty as a significant achievement. In recognition of the role of civil society and grassroot activism in the treaty's passage, the ICAN was awarded with the 2017 Nobel Peace Prize for its 'ground-breaking efforts to achieve a treaty-based prohibition of nuclear weapons.'[74] The TPNW has entered into force on 22 January 2021 and its effectiveness in terms of strengthening the norm against nuclear weapons remains to be seen. Tariq Rauf said,[75]

> The TPNW was negotiated under a mandate from the UN General Assembly and has been adopted [and] supported by 122 States. Thus it is a legitimate international treaty, even though the nine nuclear-armed States and their allies boycotted the negotiations and these States continue to reject the TPNW as impractical. The states relying on nuclear weapons for security should be encouraged to attend as Observers the first review conference of the TPNW scheduled to be held prior to January 2022 and there should a civil dialogue with TPNW States.

The main challenge for TPNW is that it lies in the low number of its signatures and ratifications compared to those of the NPT. Fact of the matter is that not only all NWS and their allies, but also many states technically capable to produce nuclear weapons have not joined the treaty. Thus TPNW yet failed to build bridges between the opposing views. As part of an effort to build bridges between parties with opposing views, the Japanese government established the 'Group of Eminent Persons for Substantive Advancement of Nuclear Disarmament,' and submitted its recommendations to the second session of the PrepCom for the 2020 NPT Review Conference.[76] The above efforts suggest that the civil society efforts on the one hand succeeded in building coalition with governments to raise the disarmament agenda thereby resulting into some significant treaties and resolutions while on the other hand failed to bridge divide between NWS and NNWS on disarmament agenda. The section below builds analysis on the effectiveness of the civil society efforts and their future role.

Effectiveness of civil society in pushing the cause of disarmament

The question of how effective or ineffective the humanitarian movements had been to promote disarmament cause is highly contested. Some view[77] these humanitarian initiatives as inconsequential in terms of influencing outcomes in the state-centric realist order while others[78] praise such initiatives reinvigorating the cause of nuclear disarmament and sensitizing the international community about it.

A balanced analysis, however, suggests that the significance of the role of civil society in relation to the nuclear disarmament lies somewhere in between the two positions.

The humanitarian normative approaches played a significant role in constructing norms against the WMD during and after the Cold War era. Despite obstacles, humanitarian activists have been able to form a very substantial global movement for nuclear disarmament. By drawing upon millions of people around the world, they have fostered nuclear arms control and disarmament measures, chilled the enthusiasm of national leaders for waging nuclear war, and pushed the idea of nuclear abolition to the forefront of the international political stage. We can observe various waves of the anti-nuclear protests such as first in the late 1940s and, second in the late 1950s and early 1960s.While the activism saw a downward trend in early 1970s,[79] in the years between 1975 and 1978 the nuclear disarmament movement once again gained vibrancy across the globe. In this timeframe, few important political developments such as the end of Vietnam War, the rise of environmentalism, the meeting of First Special Session of the UN General Assembly on Disarmament, which resulted in an agreed outcome reflecting global consensus on some principles and a way forward and the deterioration in US-Soviet relations, played a significant role in revival of civil society.[80]

Civil society brought disarmament objectives to the attention of governments and, public and concomitantly acted as a contributor in the progress on issues such as banning anti-personnel landmines, and cluster munitions based on the humanitarian approach. The joint efforts by the civil society actors and the national governments assisted in finalizing the Mine Ban Treaty and Cluster Munitions Convention.[81] Less formally, utilizing a considerable tactical toolbox, the NGOs and civil society kept alive the hope for a CTBT and worked closely with governments, scientists and officials to develop verification solutions and create the conditions that enabled the CD to bring the CTBT to conclusion.[82]

Significantly, these developments laid the foundation upon which the ATT was achieved through a partnership between progressive governments and global civil society from all regions of the world, mobilized by the Control Arms Coalition.[83] The successful engagement of the Control Arms Coalition and its partners with the ATT negotiation process confirms that transnational civil society networks continue to play an increasingly important role in global issues, particularly in the human security area. Moreover, the case study suggests that successful civil society engagement in disarmament diplomacy is not like the

Ottawa and Oslo Processes,[84] where states negotiated a free-standing treaty outside the UN, but can also be a feature of inclusive UN member state processes, where negotiations occur within formal institutions. Importantly, the ATT case suggests an enhanced role for the UN General Assembly in disarmament and arms control policy in the future and a greater openness on the part of the General Assembly to the participation of civil society. It suggests that civil society can influence complex human security issues.[85]

Indeed, these are certainly major accomplishments, and they should not be ignored in analysing the effectiveness of civil society towards nuclear disarmament. However, in broader terms, the humanitarian approaches faced severe challenges in achieving the goal towards general and complete elimination of nuclear weapons. In fact, the gap between NWS and NNWS has widened in the recent times. The fact of matter is that the realization of this vision is dependent on detailed deliberations of numerous tough realities that exist out there (discussed below).

Competing approaches – identifying the real gaps

The goal of nuclear weapons-free world has encouraged the negotiation processes and practices towards disarmament and arms control. Nevertheless, many foundations put their money elsewhere or focused exclusively on narrow parts of the nuclear puzzle. Some NGOs were overtly hostile to the efforts of the NWS to focus on the conditions enabling nuclear disarmament. Other NGO-based disarmament advocates argue that there is too much realism guiding nuclear policy.[86] However, it is important to understand that civil society put ever more emphasis on advocacy than analysis and remained less interested in political and technical matters of nuclear policy, which cannot be wished away for any real progress to be achieved. Some of the challenges and gaps in this regard are briefly discussed below.

Political obstacles

Notwithstanding the momentum for nuclear disarmament generated as a result of tremendous efforts invested by advocates of nuclear arms control and disarmament, humanitarian approaches are faced with several political and technical objectives which have to be addressed for the realization of the goal of complete nuclear abolition.

First and foremost is the challenge of differing perceptions of nuclear weapons between the proponents of the humanitarian initiatives on the one hand and the nuclear possessor and nuclear umbrella states on the other. While the proponents of the humanitarian initiatives view nuclear weapons as repugnant and focus on the humanitarian consequences of any use of these weapons, the nuclear possessor states, as well as countries under extended deterrence, continue to regard these weapons as the ultimate means to safeguard sovereignty and national security. They view them as a means to ensure peace and stability in an anarchical international system. With a few exceptions, where states have pursued nuclear capabilities driven by status motivation, a majority of the nuclear possessor states have real national security concerns which are used to justify the continuous possession of nuclear weapons by these states.

While the first group, the proponents of the humanitarian initiatives for nuclear abolition, strive for immediate banning of nuclear weapons, the second group, the possessor states and beneficiaries of extended deterrence, take the position that disarmament must follow a step-by-step approach involving interim and parallel efforts for nuclear risk reduction, confidence building, settlement of regional disputes and other challenges to regional and global security. The second group of states views the approach of the first group, which disregards the very real security threats forcing states to rely on nuclear deterrence as idealistic and impractical.

The TPNW expresses the determination of its state parties to act towards the objective of achieving effective progress towards general and complete disarmament under strict and effective international control. It views the TPNW's legally binding prohibition of nuclear weapons as an important contribution towards the achievement and maintenance of a world free of nuclear weapons, including the irreversible, verifiable and transparent elimination of nuclear weapons.[87] However, the treaty leaves unanswered several questions regarding the process from the prohibition to the eventual elimination of nuclear weapons. For example, how the process would address the underlying security concerns that push states to rely on nuclear weapons for self-defence. What will be the mechanism to ensure that any immediate prohibition on nuclear weapons on humanitarian grounds will not place any states or a group of states at a military advantage vis-à-vis other states thus exacerbating the security concerns of the latter. The outcome document of the SSOD-I, reflecting consensus of the international community on nuclear disarmament modalities, provides for proportionate reductions in a step-by-step manner while ensuring that at no stage of the disarmament process no state or a group of states is placed at an advantage vis-à-vis other states).[88]

While tremendous effort has been invested by the proponents of the humanitarian approach towards abolition, it is felt that these lobbies have shied away from similar other challenges of great practical import. There has hardly been any debate for an alternate system for ensuring to address asymmetries in non-nuclear military forces, collective security mechanisms and the significance of parallel work on mechanism for settlement of outstanding regional disputes and reviving and strengthening the role of the UN therein.

Resultantly, beyond the general agreement on the desirability of achieving one day a world free of nuclear weapons, there is no consensus on any practical roadmap for reaching complete nuclear disarmament.

Having entered into force at a time witnessing the re-emergence of multipolar strategic competition (discussed in the subsequent chapter) between NWS, marked by new race for modernization of nuclear weapons and their delivery systems, it can be argued that the TPNW appears to be disconnected with the contemporary realities.

At another level, the approach of the proponents of the TPNW has been criticized as having erected a parallel structure that undermines the existing consensus on disarmament, as enshrined in the NPT. NWS and many NATO members have opposed the TPNW from the outset. The opponents of the TPNW view the treaty is diverting attention from other disarmament and non-proliferation initiatives, such as negotiating an FMCT or ratifying the CTBT.[89] They have expressed concern that the nuclear prohibition treaty could undermine the NPT and the extensive safeguard provisions of the IAEA. The NPT NWS have continued to reiterate their commitment to their obligation under Article VI of the NPT, they have severely criticized the TPNW and in their official statements have reaffirmed the salience of nuclear weapons in their national security. It can, therefore, be argued that the humanitarian approach to abolition has widened the gap between the NWS and NNWS rather than bridging it.

At a time when the integrity of the non-proliferation regime is threatened by the actions of countries like Iran and North Korea, an NPT breakout country, giving rise to speculations about possible review of nuclear policies by other states of the Middle East and East Asia, it is all the more important to getting the non-proliferation issue right. Any suspicion and doubts about the reliability of the NPT-centric non-proliferation regime in preventing or reversing the proliferators is going to greatly undermine the hopes for nuclear disarmament. Already the fierce opponents of global zero in the US are bolstering their arguments against CTBT ratification, for example, on grounds that the US should not lower its nuclear guard at a time when the non-proliferation regime is proving to be powerless to stop the spread of nuclear weapons to determined proliferators.[90]

In connection with the above, it would also be pertinent to point out that the establishment of a nuclear-weapon-free zone (NWFZ) in the Middle East had been one of the bargains resulting in the indefinite extension of the NPT in 1995. While the TPNW reaffirms the conviction that the establishment of the internationally recognized NWFZ would enhance global and regional peace and security, strengthen the non-proliferation regime and contribute towards realizing the objective of nuclear disarmament, several proponents of the TPNW themselves have not been very steadfast in terms of demonstrating their commitment to the Middle East NWFZ. Due to political considerations their support for such a zone has never gone beyond rhetoric. Several of them have pandered to the machinations of those states which have sought to deflect the issue of the Middle East NWFZ as was evidenced in the context of debates on the follow-up to the 2010 NPT Review Conference on holding an international conference on the issue.[91] This raises questions about their altruistic commitment to the cause of disarmament. Moreover, a number of the TPNW supporter states, which are also members of the NSG, voted in favour of the 2008 NSG exemption granted to India for nuclear trade despite the non-acceptance of the IAEA Comprehensive Safeguards by India. Such exemptions while undermining the credibility of the non-proliferation regime raise doubts about the degree of altruism underpinning the global disarmament efforts. Similar observation can be made about the acquiescence of these states in the CD to the preference of the NWS commence negotiations on an FMCT which only bans the future production of fissile materials for nuclear weapons rather than accounting for the existing huge stockpiles of the nuclear weapon usable material which is imperative for any true global progress on nuclear disarmament.

Technical obstacles

Apart from the political challenges discussed above, the proponents of the humanitarian approach have also been criticized in that they have failed to consider and provide answers to various critical technical challenges which stand in the way of ensuring that any agreement on nuclear prohibition and dismantlement will be effectively and internationally verifiable. The technical challenges related to disarmament verification are still largely unaddressed. An effective international technical verification mechanism, that earns the overwhelming confidence of the international community, is imperative for developing and sustaining consensus on nuclear disarmament.

Among the several technical issues related to nuclear disarmament, the foremost relates to the process of verification of dismantlement of the weapons. While the US and the Russian Federation have some experience in terms of verification of nuclear weapons dismantlement pursuant to their bilateral agreements, many of the national technical means for verification employed by these two states are not available at the international level. While the IAEA has extensive experience in terms of verifying the non-diversion of declared nuclear material from peaceful nuclear activities, the expertise and technologies required for nuclear weapon dismantlement verification have been beyond its remit. Moreover, nuclear disarmament verifications might also require inspection of facilities and infrastructure specific to the development of nuclear weapons for which the current IAEA inspections regime is not geared. Further complicating the issue of verification of dismantlement of nuclear weapons and weapon-specific facilities will be the question of access for international inspectors to proliferation sensitive information. While NWS will be justified in denying such access on the one hand, on the other hand, any disarmament steps without effective international control and oversight would always be subject to suspicion. To what extent non-intrusive verification techniques have been developed or can inspire the confidence of the international community is yet an unanswered question.

The fundamental challenges related to nuclear disarmament verification include the issue of assurances regarding the non-existence of undeclared weapons and related facilities. Once a state has decided to disarm and then successfully dismantled its nuclear infrastructure, how would it be able to provide assurances to other states that the process was complete? It would need to convince them that there was no plutonium, highly enriched uranium or nuclear explosive devices hidden away somewhere. The international community's track record in finding undeclared nuclear activities using the IAEA's authority enhanced under the IAEA Additional Protocol is not very encouraging, and the agency itself has admitted that the tools at its disposal are insufficient in the face of determined concealment.[92]

In a world in which all nuclear weapons are finally banned, the system of monitoring and inspections will be the primary barrier to nuclear breakout and resumed arms competition. Nuclear technology, materials and knowledge will continue to be present around the globe in civilian programs. As more and more states develop capacity, there will always be the possibility of attempts by states to divert the technology and know-how towards the development of the nuclear weapons. This would necessitate verification and detection mechanism that is continuously and indefinitely effective and has the confidence of the international community. Such a mechanism will have to go beyond the existing IAEA authority to ensure that nuclear weapons-related activities, not necessarily involving nuclear materials are also effectively detected and countered. Both the Democratic People's Republic of Korea and Iran cases demonstrate the challenges of ensuring such a verification regime. A nuclear zero verification regime would require a margin of zero error.

Another issue that will have to be taken on while negotiating a nuclear zero regime will be the right of states to possess complete national fuel cycles. Whereas the spread of complete fuel cycle capabilities will definitely intensify the threat of latent nuclear weapons programs, presenting further challenges to nuclear disarmament verification, it should not be expected that in the context of negotiations on a truly non-discriminatory disarmament regime the NNWS would allow the perpetuation of the privileges and monopoly presently enjoyed by the NWS over certain aspects of nuclear technology. A new bargain on general and complete nuclear disarmament would not be possible without doing away with the current discriminatory order defined by the NPT.

The breakout problem

While the proponents of the humanitarian approach have rushed to finalize the TPNW calling for immediate prohibition on nuclear weapons, they seem to have given a little thought to the challenges of breakouts from the treaty. Even if all the nuclear possessor states were to join the TPNW today and resultantly dismantle their nuclear weapons leading to a world free of nuclear weapons, the preceding discussion on the challenges of verification underscores the need to think about the day after.

There is no mechanism in the TPNW to deal with violations. What will be the mechanism for other parties to respond to a violation after it has been detected, and the degree to which parties face incentives to cheat in the first place? The treaty also does not provide any plan of action to dissuade states from acquiring nuclear weapons by exploiting the space generated after the disarmament of all others in order to claim itself the only nuclear weapons power. Has any thinking been done about the humanitarian impact of a breakout state capitalizing on its nuclear weapons as instruments of extortion or mass extermination? It does not consider the impact of a treaty violation on the military balance and the humanitarian catastrophes which could ensue from possible misadventures of militarily advanced states in the absence of nuclear deterrence. No mechanism is provided for widespread and effective defences or a system whereby, in the event of violation, former nuclear weapons powers would be able to quickly reconstitute countervailing deterrent or reprisal forces.

To sum up, the technical and political obstacles that confront proponents of nuclear disarmament are multifaceted and severe. The civil society campaigns towards nuclear disarmament have not taken these realities into serious considerations while promoting immediate ban on nuclear weapons on humanitarian ground. Though the entry into force of the TPNW could be considered as a step towards strengthening the international norm against nuclear weapons, to what extent it can be construed as constituting a part or contributing to the development of customary international law is highly debatable given the consistent and unequivocal statements to the contrary of all nuclear possessor states.

Conclusion

Historic progress in the field of nuclear disarmament has been due to shared efforts of civil society movements and political forces that have relied on a delicate balance of idealism and realism. On the one hand, disarmament debate is indeed justified on humanitarian ground as nuclear weapons are catastrophic and against humanity and civilization. This notion is grounded in foundation of ethics, morality and international law. Yet on the other hand, justification for nuclear weapons rests on its substantive practical merits in guaranteeing states' genuine national security needs.

Despite strong security-centric position held by NWS, humanitarian activists and disarmament movements succeeded to generate awareness at the grassroots level, mobilizing civil society movements at the regional and global level and by building larger coalition with governments to promote the disarmament agenda. By drawing upon millions of people around the world, civil society groups have pushed the idea of nuclear abolition to the forefront of the international political stage. The civil society brought disarmament objectives to the attention of governments and public on issues such as banning anti-personnel landmines, cluster munitions and implementation of the NPT with respect to prohibition of nuclear tests. The joint efforts by civil society actors and the national governments assisted in finalizing the Mine Ban Treaty and Cluster Munitions Convention thereby creating the conditions that enabled the CD to bring the CTBT to conclusion.[93]

That said, the ATT was achieved through a partnership between progressive governments and global civil society from all regions of the world, mobilized by the Control Arms Coalition.[94] The successful engagement of the Control Arms Coalition and its partners with the ATT negotiation process confirms that transnational civil society networks continue to play an increasingly important role in global issues, particularly in the human security area. Importantly, the ATT case suggests an enhanced role for the UN General Assembly in disarmament and arms control policy in the future and a greater openness on the part of the General Assembly to the participation of civil society. It suggests that civil society can influence complex human security issues.[95]

The humanitarian initiative championed mainly by ICAN, affiliated groups, and numerous governments successfully led to the conclusion of TPNW. The proponents view (as highlighted above) the TPNW's legally binding prohibition of nuclear weapons as an important contribution towards the achievement and maintenance of a world free of nuclear weapons, including the irreversible, verifiable and transparent elimination of nuclear weapons. However, the treaty leaves set of unanswered questions regarding the process from the prohibition to the eventual elimination of nuclear weapons. The TPNW disregards the underlying security concerns that push states to rely on nuclear weapons. There has hardly been any debate for an alternate system for ensuring addressing asymmetries in non-nuclear military forces, collective security mechanisms and the significance of parallel work on mechanism for settlement of outstanding regional disputes and reviving and strengthening the role of the UN therein. Notwithstanding the momentum for nuclear disarmament generated as a result of tremendous efforts invested by advocates of nuclear disarmament, humanitarian approaches are faced with several political and technical hurdles which have to be addressed for the realization of the goal of complete nuclear abolition.

The opponents of the TPNW expressed concern that the nuclear prohibition treaty could undermine the NPT and the extensive safeguard provisions of the IAEA. They view the treaty as diverting attention from other disarmament and non-proliferation initiatives, such as negotiating an FMCT or ratifying the CTBT.[96] The NWS and some other NATO states have criticized the TPNW while reaffirming the salience of nuclear weapons in their national security. It can, therefore, be argued that the humanitarian approach to abolition has widened the gap between the NWS and NNWS rather than bridging it. There seems no consensus between NWS and NNWS on any practical roadmap for reaching complete nuclear disarmament. The formula for sustaining and expanding this progress will require persistent cooperation and coordination to overcome differing perceptions of nuclear weapons between the proponents of the humanitarian initiatives on the one hand and the nuclear possessor and nuclear umbrella states on the other. How gaps between the above competing approaches be bridged is discussed in the subsequent chapters.

Notes

1. Christopher A. Ford, 'Debating Disarmament: Interpreting Article VI of the Treaty on the Non-Proliferation of Nuclear Weapons,' *Nonproliferation Review,* Vol. 14, No. 3 (November 2007), p. 401.
2. Rebecca Davis Gibbons, 'The Humanitarian Turn in Nuclear Disarmament and the Treaty on the Prohibition Nuclear Weapons,' *The Nonproliferation Review,* Vol. 25, No. 01 (July 2018), p.12.
3. Daryl G. Kimball, 'Nuclear Disarmament and Humans Survival,' *Arms Control Association* (2014): https://www.armscontrol.org/act/2014_01-02/Focus.
4. Matashichi Oishi, 'The Fisherman,' in Nic Maclellan (ed.), *Grappling with the Bomb Britain's Pacific H-bomb Tests* (Australian National University Press, 2017), pp. 55–68.
5. Wolfgang Rudig, *Anti-nuclear Movements: A World Survey of Opposition to Nuclear Energy* (Harlow, Essex: Longman Current Affairs, 1990), pp. 54–55.
6. Jim Falk, *Global Fission: The Battle over Nuclear Power* (New York: Oxford University Press, 1982), pp. 96–97.
7. See 'The Russell-Einstein Manifesto', *Student Pugwash Michigan* (July 9, 1955): http://umich.edu/~pugwash/Manifesto.html.
8. Ibid.
9. See 'History,' *Pugwash Conferences on Science and World Affairs*: https://pugwash.org/history/.
10. Joseph Rotblat, 'The Pugwash Conferences on Science and World Affairs,' *Medicine and War,* Vol. 1, No. 1 (1985), pp. 51–54: https://doi.org/10.1080/07488008508408608.
11. Jacek Kuśmierek, and Anna Płachcińska, 'A Contribution of Józef Rotblat, a Winner of the Nobel Peace Prize, to the Development of Nuclear Medicine,' *Nuclear Medicine Review,* Vol. 22, No. 2 (2019), p. 97.
12. J. B. Priestley, 'Britain and the Nuclear Bomb,' *New Statesman* (February 12, 2007): https://www.newstatesman.com/society/2007/02/nuclear-world-britain-power.
13. See 'Who we are,' *Campaign for Nuclear Disarmament,*': https://cnduk.org/who/.

14. Henry J. Steck, 'The Re-Emergence of Ideological Politics in Great Britain: the Campaign for Nuclear Disarmament,' *Political Research Quarterly*, Vol. 18, No. 1 (1965), p. 87: https://doi.org/10.1177% 2F106591296501800108.

15. Jenny Pickerill and Frank Webster, 'The Anti-War/ Peace Movement in Britain and the Conditions of Information War,' *International Relations,* Vol. 20, No. 04 (2006), p. 407.

16. See 'Origins,' *Bertrand Russell Peace Foundation*: http://www.russfound.org/about/about.htm.

17. Ibid.

18. See Patrick Burke, 'European Nuclear Disarmament: Transnational Peace Campaigning in the 1980s' in Eckart Conze, Martin Klimke, & Jeremy Varon (eds.), *Nuclear Threats, Nuclear Fear and the Cold War of the 1980s* (Cambridge: Cambridge University, 2016), pp. 227–250; and Peter Baehr, 'E.P. Thompson and European Nuclear Disarmament (END): A Critical Retrospective,' *The Online Journal of and Conflict Resolution*, No. 2.5/3.1 (March 2000).

19. See 'Philip Noel-Baker,' *The Nobel Prize*: https://www.nobelprize.org/prizes/peace/1959/noel-baker/facts/.

20. Alex Poteliakhoff, 'The Rise and Fall Professions for World Disarmament and Development,' *Medicine, Conflict and Survival,* Vol. 24, No. 03 (July–September 2008), pp. 188–189: https://doi.org/10.1080/13623690802169894.

21. See 'About Abolition 2000,' *Abolition 2000: Global Network to Eliminate Nuclear Weapons*: http://www.abolition2000.org/en/about/abolition-2000/.

22. Ibid.

23. Carah Ong, 'The Growing Danger of a Nuclear Middle East,' *Middle East Report*, No. 247 (Summer 2008): https://merip.org/2008/06/the-growing-danger-of-a-nuclear-middle-east/.

24. Ben Ter Veer, 'The Struggle against the Deployment of Cruise Missiles: The Learning Process of the Dutch Peace Movement,' *Bulletin of Peace Proposals,* Vol. 19, No. 02 (1988), p. 214: https://doi.org/10.1177 %2F096701068801900210.

25. Philip P. Everts, 'The Churches and Attitudes on Nuclear Weapons: The Case of the Netherlands,' *Bulletin of Peace Proposals,* Vol. 15, No. 03 (1984), p. 229: https://doi.org/10.1177%2F096701068401500306.

26. See 'IPPNW: A Brief History,' *International Physicians for the Prevention of Nuclear War*: https://www.ippnw.org/about/ippnw-a-brief-history.

27. Frank M. Castillo, 'The International Physicians for the Prevention of Nuclear War: Transnational Midwife of World Peace,' *Medicine and War,* Vol. 6, No. 4 (1990), p. 255: http://www.tandfonline.com/action/showCitFormats?doi=10.1080/07488009008408945.

28. See 'IPPNW: A Brief History,'.

29. See 'About Us,' *Nuclear Age Peace Foundation*: https://www.wagingpeace.org/about/.

30. See 'The Marshall Islands' Nuclear Zero Cases in the International Court of Justice: Background and Current Status Lawyers Committee on Nuclear Policy/April 2016,' *The Lawyers Committee on Nuclear Policy Inc.*: http://lcnp.org/RMI/.

31. Ibid.

32. See 'The Campaign,' *International Campaign to Abolish Nuclear Weapons (ICAN)*: https://www.icanw.org/the_campaign.
33. See 'The Nobel Peace Prize for 2017,' *The Nobel Prize*: https://www.nobelprize.org/prizes/peace/2017/press-release/.
34. Daryl Kimball 'The Ottawa Convention at a Glance,' *Arms Control Association,* (2018): https://www.armscontrol.org/factsheets/ottawa.
35. See *Beyond War Communicator's Guide* (Palo Alto, California: 1985): http://traubman.igc.org/bwguide.pdf.
36. Susan Rice and Nancy L. Mary, *'Beyond War: A New Perspective for Social Work,' Social Work,* Vol. 34, No. 02 (March 1989), p. 176: https://www.jstor.org/stable/23715797.
37. Susan D. Macafee, 'History of the Ribbon,' *The Ribbon International* (August 11, 2015): https://historyoftheribbon.blogspot.com/2015/08/by-susan-d.html.
38. See 'Alliance for Nuclear Accountability,': https://ananuclear.org/about/.
39. See 'Great Peace March for Global Nuclear Disarmament Records (DG 147),' *Swarthmore College for Peace Collection*: https://www.swarthmore.edu/library/peace/DG100-150/DG147/DG147GPM.htm.
40. See 'Parliamentarians for Nuclear Non-Proliferation and Disarmament (PNND),' *Basel Peace Office*: https://www.baselpeaceoffice.org/article/parliamentarians-nuclear-non-proliferation-and-disarmament-pnnd.
41. See 'Humanitarian Disarmament,': https://humanitariandisarmament.org/about/.
42. See 'Resolution Adopted by General Assembly on 5 December 2013,' *United Nations General Assembly* (December 10, 2013): https://undocs.org/A/RES/68/32.
43. Kathleen Lawand, 'ICRC: Is the World Ready to Face a Nuclear War? No. So Let's Ban the Bomb,' *International Committee of the Red Cross* (February 11, 2019): https://www.icrc.org/en/document/icrc-world-ready-face-nuclear-war-no-so-lets-ban-bomb.
44. Dimity Hawkins, 'Now e can: Civil Society and Governments Moving toward a Ban on Nuclear Weapons,' in *Disarmament Forum,* Vol. 4 (2010), p. 39: https://www.peacepalacelibrary.nl/ebooks/files/UNIDIR_pdf-art3021.pdf.
45. Gibbons, 'The Humanitarian Turn,' pp. 11 and 25.
46. Tariq Rauf, 'The 2000 NPT Review Conference: Challenges and Prospects,' *James Martin Center for Non-proliferation Studies*: https://nonproliferation.org/wp-content/uploads/2016/06/21apr00.pdf.
47. Raj Kumar Kothari, 'Russia's Policy toward Nuclear Disarmament: A Theoretical Framework,' in *Nuclear Disarmament: Regional Perspectives,* Vol. 21 (Emerald Group Publishing Limited, 2013), p. 94.
48. Jayantha Dhanapala, 'Multilateralism and the Future of the Global Nuclear Nonproliferation Regime,' *The Nonproliferation Review* (Fall 2001), 6.
49. These NGOs are Albert Schweitzer Institute, Basel Peace Office, Global Security Institute, International Association of Lawyers Against Nuclear Arms, International Network of Engineers and Scientists for Global Responsibility, International Peace Bureau, Nuclear Age Peace Foundation, and Parliamentarians for Nuclear Nonproliferation and Disarmament.

50. See 'About Middle Power Initiative,': http://www.middlepowers.org/oldwebsite/about.html.
51. See 'Report of the Canberra Commission of the Elimination of the Nuclear Weapons,' (Canberra: National Capital Printers, 1996): https://www.dfat.gov.au/sites/default/files/the-canberra-commission-on-the-elimination-of-nuclear-weapons.pdf.
52. See 'Facing Nuclear Dangers: An Action Plan for the 21st Century, The Report of the Tokyo Forum for Nuclear Non-Proliferation and Disarmament,' *Japan Institute of International Affairs Hiroshima Peace Institute* (July 25, 1999).
53. Randy Rydell, 'Security through Disarmament: The Story of the Weapons of Mass Destruction Commission,' *The Hague Journal of Diplomacy,* Vol. 2, No. 1 (2007), pp. 81–91.
54. Hans Blix, *Weapons of Terror: Freeing the World of Nuclear, Biological and Chemical Arms* (Stockholm: EO GrafisKa, 2006), p. 14.
55. See Rebecca Johnson, 'The United Nations and Disarmament Treatise,' *United Nations UN Chronicle*: https://www.un.org/en/chronicle/article/united-nations-and-disarmament-treaties.
56. 'Shultz, Perry, Kissinger, Nun Call for New, Safer and More Stable Form of Deterrence,' *Carnegie Corporation of New York* (July 3, 2011): https://www.carnegie.org/news/articles/shultz-perry-kissinger-nunn-call-for-new-safer-and-more-stable-form-of-deterrence/.
57. George P. Shultz, William J. Perry, Henry A. Kissinger, 'A World Free of Nuclear Weapons' *The Wall Street Journal* (January 4, 2008).
58. George P. Shultz, William J. Perry, Henry A. Kissinger, 'Toward a World without Nuclear Weapons,' *The Wall Street Journal* (January 15, 2007).
59. Andrea Berger and Malcolm Chalmers, 'The Art of the Possible: The Future of the P5 Process On Nuclear Weapons,' *Arms Control Association* (October 2014): https://www.armscontrol.org/act/2014-10/features/art-possible-future-p5-process-nuclear-weapons#one.
60. Tariq Rauf, 'Visions of Butterflies and Unicorns as the Nuclear Disarmament Architecture Collapses: The Final Session of the Preparatory Committee for the 2020 Non-Proliferation Treaty Review Conference,' *Journal of Strategic Affairs* (2019), p. 3.
61. See 'Non-Proliferation and Disarmament Initiatives (NPDI),' *Nuclear Threat Initiative* (May 31, 2020): https://www.nti.org/learn/treaties-and-regimes/non-proliferation-and-disarmament-initiative-npdi/.
62. See 'Nuclear Disarmament and Resource Collection,' *Nuclear Threat Initiative* (December 15, 2020): https://www.nti.org/analysis/reports/nuclear-disarmament/.
63. Tom Sauer, 'The NPT and Humanitarian Initiative: Towards and Beyond the 2015 NPT Review Conference,' *Deep Cuts Working Paper,* No. 5 (2015), p. 7.
64. Gibbons, 'Nuclear Disarmament,' pp. 1–2.
65. See 'Vienna Conference on the Humanitarian Impact of Nuclear Weapons 8–9 Dec, 2014,' *Federal Ministry Republic of Austria, European and International Affairs*: https://www.bmeia.gv.at/en/european-foreign-policy/disarmament/weapons-of-mass-destruction/nuclear-weapons/vienna-conference-on-the-humanitarian-impact-of-nuclear-weapons/.

66. See Sebastian Kurz, 'Joint Statement on Behalf of the Humanitarian Impact of Nuclear Weapons at the 2015 NPT Review Conference,' (April 28, 2015): https://www.mofa.go.jp/files/000079082.pdf.
67. Alexander Kmentt, 'The Development of the International Initiative on the Humanitarian Impact of Nuclear Weapons and its effect on Nuclear Weapons Debate,' *International Review of the Red Cross,* Vol. 97 (2015), pp. 682–683: doi:10.1017/S1816383116000059.
68. Rizwana Abbasi, 'Creating an Environment for Nuclear Disarmament,' *E-International Relations* (August 2, 2019): https://www.e-ir.info/2019/08/02/creating-an-environment-for-nuclear-disarmament/.
69. Ann Linde, 'Swedish Initiative Aims to Strengthen the NPT,' *Arms Control Association* (March 2020): https://www.armscontrol.org/act/2020-03/features/swedish-initiative-aims-strengthen-npt.
70. Heather Williams, 'A Nuclear Babel: Narratives around the Treaty on the Prohibition of Nuclear Weapons,' *The Nonproliferation Review,* Vol. 25, No. 1–2 (2018), p. 1.
71. See 'Treaty Banning Nuclear Weapons Opens for Signature at UN,' *UN News* (September 20, 2017): https://news.un.org/en/story/2017/09/565582-treaty-banning-nuclear-weapons-opens-signature-un.
72. Michael Hamel-Green, 'The Nuclear Ban Treaty and 2018 Disarmament Forums: An initial Impact Assessment,' *Journal for Peace and Nuclear Disarmament,* Vol. 1, No. 2 (2018), p. 445.
73. Author's Interview with Asif Durrani.
74. Billy Perrigo, 'How the World is Reacting to ICAN Winning the Nobel Peace Prize,' *TIME* (6 0ctober, 2017): https://time.com/4972021/nobel-peace-prize-2017-ican-reacts/.
75. Author's interview with Tariq Rauf.
76. See 'Group of Eminent Persons for Substantive Advancement of Nuclear Disarmament,' *Ministry of Foreign Affairs of Japan* (April 16, 2019): https://www.mofa.go.jp/dns/ac_d/page25e_000178.html.
77. Tytti Erästö, 'The NPT and the TPNW: Compatible or Conflicting Nuclear Weapons Treaties?,' *SIPRI* (March 6, 2019): https://www.sipri.org/commentary/blog/2019/npt-and-tpnw-compatible-or-conflicting-nuclear-weapons-treaties.
78. Ibid.
79. Lawrence S. Wittner, 'The Forgotten Years of the World Nuclear Disarmament Movement, 1975-78,' *Journal of Peace Research,* Vol. 40, No. 4 (2003), p. 436.
80. Ibid., p. 451.
81. See Richard Price, 'Reversing the Gun Sights: Transnational Civil Society Targets Landmines,' *International Organization,* Vol. 53, No. 3 (Summer 1998), pp. 613–644; Maxwell A. Cameron, Robert J. Lawson and Brain W. Tomlin (ed.), *To Walk without Fear: The Global Movement to Ban Landmines* (Toronto: Oxford University Press, 1998); and Jhon Borrie, *Unacceptable Harm: A History of How the Treaty to Ban Cluster Munitions Was Won,* Vol. 8 (Geneva: UNIDIR Publications, 2009): https://unidir.org/files/publications/pdfs/unacceptable-harm-a-history-of-how-the-treaty-to-ban-cluster-munitions-was-won-en-258.pdf.

82. See Rebecca Johnson, 'Civil Society and the Conference on Disarmament,' *UNIDIR Resources* (February, 2011), p. 1: https://www.unidir.org/files/publications/pdfs/civil-society-and-the-conference-on-disarmament-360.pdf.

83. See Robert Perkins, 'Civil Society Remains Vital to Success of Arms Control Processes,' *UNA-UK,* https://una.org.uk/7-civil-society-remains-vital-success-arms-control-processes.

84. Nicola Short, 'The Role of NGOs in the Ottawa Process to Ban Landmines,' *International Negotiation,* Vol. 4, No. 3 (January 01, 1999), pp. 481–500.

85. Helena Whall and Allison Pytlak, 'The Role of Civil Society in the International Negotiations on the Arms Trade Treaty,' *Global Policy,* Vol. 5, No. 4 (November, 2014), p. 465.

86. Brad Roberts, 'On Creating the Conditions for Nuclear Disarmament: Past Lessons, Future Prospects,' *The Washington Quarterly,* Vol. 42, No. 2 (Summer 2019), p. 20.

87. See 'Treaty on the Prohibition of the Nuclear Weapons,' *United Nations Office for Disarmament Affairs* (2017), pp. 10–11: https://www.un.org/disarmament/wp-content/uploads/2017/10/tpnw-info-kit-v2.pdf.

88. See Daryl Kimball, 'The Treaty on the Prohibition of Nuclear Weapons at a Glance,' *Arms Control Association* (January 2021): https://www.armscontrol.org/factsheets/nuclearprohibition

89. Ibid.

90. Ibid.

91. Kelsey Davenport, 'WMD-Free Middle East Proposal at a Glance,' *Arms Control Association* (December 2018): https://www.armscontrol.org/factsheets/mewmdfz.

92. Ford, 'Why Not Nuclear Disarmament?,' pp. 8–9.

93. See Johnson, 'Civil Society and the Conference on Disarmament,' p. 1.

94. See Perkins, 'Civil Society Remains Vital,'.

95. Whall and Pytlak, 'The Role of Civil Society,' p. 465.

96. See Kimball 'The Treaty on the Prohibition of Nuclear Weapons.'

3 Contemporary security environment

New technologies and nuclear disarmament

Introduction

Inter-state military competition has been intensifying globally in the recent years. For example, in Europe, NATO partners are anxious to meet Russia's military resurgence, its disruptive cross-domain coercive plans,[1] and its growing anti-access area denial (A2/AD) capabilities which spread all the way from Kola to Kaliningrad and on to Crimea.[2] The NATO members, in turn, are reinforcing the readiness of their military forces while seeking to reestablish the credibility of their deterrence.[3] The rise of China has shifted the power balance to the Western Pacific,[4] thus influencing the US supremacy in that region. Inter-state rivalries, including North Korea-South Korea in East Asia, and India-Pakistan in South Asia, continue to spark insecurity and fuel vicious cycles of armament, both within and outside of these rivalries.

Furthermore, states' alliance politics, broken channels of communication, frequent border skirmishes in certain regions (case in point is tension between India-China and India-Pakistan) can aggravate negative[5] threat perceptions of one against the other. Employment of hybrid warfare,[6] inclusion of new technologies in their inventories, absence of risk reduction mechanisms, states' interference in others' territories through proxies,[7] insurgencies and non-states actors,[8] political rhetoric like propaganda, hate speech and competing or irreconcilable narratives breed heightened threat perceptions, driving a vicious cycle of dangerous conditions under which misunderstandings could escalate to unprecedented levels of confrontation between the nuclear powers. Moreover, the absence of CBMs[9] and the nonexistence of regional arms control dialogues have curtailed space for arms restraint. This in turn has pushed regional states towards the adoption of offensive war-fighting strategies and preemptive, counter-force postures.

DOI: 10.4324/9781003131205-3

The contemporary global political system is entering a multipolar order[10] thereby shifting large and small powers' focus away from the Atlantic and Europe to Asia, thus challenging the relevance[11] of the western-centric non-proliferation treaties. All the existing mechanisms directed to promote arms control and disarmament are in despair. Currently, states' reliance on modernization of deterrent force has increased while their emphasis on arms control and disarmament has decreased. States are focused on creating dominance in arms race, space and new technologies. These arms racing problems have created dangerous risks of accidental war, miscalculation, problems of strategic instability and disarmament crisis. The questions addressed in this chapter are: Why is the influence of nuclear weapons technologies on international security affairs so pervasive? How intensified conflicts, states' increased reliance on nuclear weapons and new technologies have aggravated the strategic instability and asymmetries globally that in turn has undermined the prospects for nuclear disarmament?

Altering nature of warfare

The nature and character of warfare has changed in the present environment. The world has witnessed four varying phases till date that suggest the altering character of weapons and the nature of warfare. The first wave evolved after the invention of nuclear technology that fundamentally altered the nature of warfare.[12] The above notions contextualize what we now refer to as Deterrence Theory.[13] The second phase emerged in the milieu of intense arms competition during the Cold War. The scholars[14] gave remedy not just for reducing risks and preventing accidents but constraining decisions that can trigger accidents.[15] The third-era thinkers focused on threat perceptions and understanding the underlying reasons that had led to crises and the mechanisms to prevent such crises. They dedicated their attention to understand the process of compromising, as a degree of compromise can prevent or resolve conflicts.[16] The two superpowers got past the brink of confrontation to enter in an era of détente. The US President Richard Nixon and Soviet leader Leonid Brezhnev pledged to permanently limit their countries' offensive nuclear arsenal. Thus, arms control mechanisms, a negotiating toolkit regulated some aspect of the US and Soviet military capabilities and somehow had stabilizing effects thereby preventing fog of war between the two superpowers. The history taught us lesson that arms control and security policy are not opposed to each other. What Schelling and Halperin noted in *Strategy and Arms Control*, is that 'arms control, if properly conceived, is not necessarily hostile to, or incompatible with, or an alternative to, a military policy properly conceived by any state.'[17]

Gradually, the fourth phase emerged after the end of the Cold War on the applicability of deterrence. In contrast to earlier theories, non-traditional threats became a primary focus of strategic thinkers.[18] The collapse of the Soviet Union brought down with it the whole military-political security agenda that had dominated world politics during the Cold War. During this phase, the events such as Kargil War in 1999, and a series of other crises[19] between nuclear possessor states demonstrated the emergence of the stability-instability paradox[20] in South Asia. Unlike the Cold War, deterrence failed to offer total peace in South Asia as peace remains fragile at the lower level of the escalation ladder.

Currently, we are witnessing the fifth wave in which deterrence has evolved in a new direction. One, at the strategic level, modernization of nuclear weapon systems, introduction of new and destabilizing weapon systems, like the hypersonic systems, ABMs and doctrinal innovations are generating insecurity and instability. Two, advancements in new technologies and threatening prospects of the militarization of cyber space, Artificial Intelligence (AI) and military applications of big data analytics, quantum computing and weaponization of outer space are transforming the nature of warfare (discussed below). However, in the renewed geo-strategic competition and military significance, states have displayed little appetite for restraints and security through arms control based on the principle of undiminished severity for all at the lowest level of armaments. Answering to a question if the present global security environment is favourable to nuclear disarmament, Durrani commented,[21]

> short answer is no. For nuclear disarmament to take place, major possessors must have some level of mutual understanding and trust to commence a process. Current geopolitical developments clearly reflect absence of any trust or understanding. Quite the opposite-growing competition and rivalry. Hence, there seem no prospects for nuclear disarmament.

Unfortunately, in the face of these threats, the UN disarmament machinery appears to have remained focused on some particular issues and anachronisms. The technology holders are averse to discussions about legally binding arrangement to prevent the weaponization of new technologies. The debates in the CD and on other types of weapons of mass destruction, discussions in the Open-Ended Working

Group and the Group of Government Experts on cyber security, and elsewhere, point towards complacency in dealing with these urgent challenges.

Thus, smarter technologies seem to be changing the course of nuclear weapons in the contemporary war theatre. Despite all these changes that have occurred, nuclear weapons still remain pervasive in the national security policies of old and new NWS. Resurgence of conflicts and new security threats have increased states' insecurities that in turn has compelled them into renewed arms competition thereby increasing their reliance on new technologies in order to fight smart wars.

Renewed great power competition

The post-Cold War era, sometimes reckoned as the unipolar world in which a dominant US-led Western coalition largely set and enforced the rules of the international order, is returning to a state of sharper and more explicit great power competition. Russia and China are actively contesting the US supremacy and alliances in Eastern Europe and East Asia. They are advancing their own vision of a multipolar order in which the US is more constrained and its power diluted. Other aspiring great powers such as Japan, South Korea, Brazil, Australia and India are also stepping up their drive for power projection. In fact, great power rivalry is again becoming a principal theme of global politics.

In this process, military capabilities enable states to defend against adversaries (acting alone or in the context of an alliance). Twenty years into the 21st century, the US, Russia and China continue to acquire hi-tech systems such as fifth-generation fighters, heavy bombers and aircraft carriers. Yet by reducing the price of precision and advanced manufacturing, the fourth industrial revolution is creating a new generation of smaller, smarter and cheaper weapons that challenges these weapons systems. We are heading to an age of mass precision. A key question in the unfolding era of great power competition is which nation can most swiftly and efficiently readjust to this revolution.

This section examines inter-state rivalries, states' competitive behaviour in the military arena through a selection of leading certain regions that are embroiled in conflictual environment. This selection includes the bilateral rivalries between states such as US-China, US-Russia, China-India, India-Pakistan and South Korea-North Korea. It proceeds with an assessment of the actual build-up of military capabilities of these states through a concise assessment of their defence expenditures, military procurement, their inclination to procure new technologies and their military research and development activities. This section assesses that how competition rather than cooperation is a recurring theme in these states' security settings which in turn affects the renewed prospects for nuclear disarmament.

Russia's threat perceptions and security environment

Russia seems to be in competition with other actors such as China, the EU and the US. Nevertheless, its insecurity essentially derives from the US and NATO supremacy in conventional weaponry, the US' modernization in nuclear weapons, space and new technologies which has led Moscow to stress its nuclear and retaliatory capabilities, thereby fuelling Western insecurity. The development such as NATO's expansion, US installation of BMD systems in Europe,[22] US invasion of Iraq,[23] its backing of colour revolutions[24] and abrogating the ABM Treaty are considered by Russia as offensive moves. Moscow considers that US deterrent force modernization[25] and rising conventional asymmetry could undermine Russia's second strike capability.[26] Whereas the US perception of Russia builds on the informational warfare and interference in 2016 presidential elections,[27] Moscow's nuclear modernization programs, Ukrainian issue, support for regimes in Syria and Venezuela, alignment with China and the poisoning of Kremlin opponents.[28] In the West, these developments are considered as fundamentally revisionist moves towards the US.

The erosion of American hegemony, instability of international institutions, abrogation of arms control agreements and return of great power rivalry all contribute to heightened uncertainties and increased potential for conflict between the US and Russia.

Russia's growing reliance on military modernization

The Russian Federation maintains a triad of nuclear forces consisting of ICBMs, SLBMs and heavy bombers and it continues to modernize all the three legs of the strategic triad. Russia's President, Vladimir Putin stated in late 2019, 'our equipment must be better than the world's best if we want to come out as winners.'[29] He reiterated, 'we will continue to strengthen our nuclear forces.'[30]

The early 2020 estimates suggest that Russia possess stockpile of 4,310 nuclear warheads to be delivered by long-range strategic launchers. Nearly 2,060 of retired but largely intact warheads await dismantlement, for a total inventory of approximately 6,370 warheads.[31] Russia's ICBM force currently comprises 302 missiles that can deliver up to

1,136 warheads, although only about 812 warheads are deployed. Over half of these delivery platforms are MIRVed.[32] Russia's Strategic Naval Forces possesses ten strategic submarines of three different types such as Delta, Typhoon and Borei. The Delta and Borei-class submarines can each carry 16 SLBMs, with multiple warheads on a missile, for a combined maximum loading of more than 720 warheads. Reportedly, Russia strategic bomber fleet (60–70) is comprised of around 50 Tu-160 (carry up to 16 AS-15) and remaining Tu-95MS (carry up to 12 AS-15) aircrafts. A newer type of the Tu-160, with enhanced stealth characteristics, has started production in 2020s; thereby adding up 50–60 aircrafts in its inventory.[33]

Russia possesses approximately 2,000 non-strategic nuclear warheads.[34] It possesses Avangard HGV that can manoeuver to evade air defences and ballistic missile defences. President Putin stated that Russia would pursue 'a new hypersonic-speed, high-precision new weapons systems that can hit targets at inter-continental distance and can adjust their altitude and course as they travel' in response to the US withdrawal from the ABM Treaty.[35] These technologies are dual-use and lead to misinterpretation. Russia has been testing the Poseidon Autonomous Underwater Vehicle where each drone would be armed with a two-megaton nuclear or conventional payload that could be detonated 'thousands of feet' below the surface.[36] Russia has been developing the Tsirkon, an anti-ship HCMs, since at least 2011. President Putin in February 2019 stated that 'the Tsirkon missile fired from surface ships or submarines can reach a speed of approximately Mach 9 (about 11,000 kph) and strike a target more than 1,000 km away underwater or on the ground.'[37] In late 2019, President Putin also noted that Russia would develop a land-based version of this missile as a response to the US withdrawal from the INF Treaty. The Tsirkon underwent testing with potential deployment around 2020.[38]

The Trump administration's abrogation of the INF Treaty came out in the backdrop of the claim that Russia has developed and fielded a missile system, the Novator 9M729, with range that violates the INF Treaty and challenges the Euro-Atlantic security. Russia, in turn, denied these charges and blamed the US for producing the Mk-41 Vertical Launching System for missile interceptors at the Aegis Ashore facility in Romania and Poland. Argument holds that the US security competition with China is a major driving factor that has encouraged the US' withdrawal from the treaty. China is not a party to this treaty, therefore, the real concerns are attached to China's growing influence, its investment in ground-based cruise and ballistic missiles, and future military modernization plans. Thus the US believes that the

INF Treaty prohibits it from acquiring and fielding more missiles and weapon systems in Asia. Tariq Rauf asserted,[39]

> over the past decade, relations between the five nuclear-weapon states have been deteriorating due to increasing political differences and rivalries, and development and deployment of advanced weapons. In addition, important treaties such as the ABM Treaty and the INF Treaty have collapsed due to US withdrawal. While New START has been extended to February 2026, prospects are not bright for a follow-on Russia-US treaty on further reductions in strategic nuclear weapons; China is not prepared to come to the table despite US insistence; and the US has been championing an initiative to 'create the conditions for nuclear disarmament' that has had a mixed response. Overall, a new Cold War is brewing and further developments in nuclear disarmament are becoming problematic.

The US withdrawal from INF has led to mistrust and insecurity within the EU.[40] Russia's arms build-up and fielding of missile systems will demand a strong NATO response, including renewed nuclear deployments by the EU states. So, the US will be compelled to install more intermediate-range missiles in Europe that in turn would destabilize the broader European region. The demise of the INF Treaty will fuel further arms race, thereby increasing the risks of accidental war, miscalculation and strategic instability not only in Europe but also in the Asia-Pacific. The arms control crisis between the US and Russia will also fuel a new arms racing problem in Asia.

New Cold War in Asia: Who challenges whom?

Currently, Asia has become the engine of future global economy.[41] Thus, the US is heavily consumed to rebalance its economic, political and security commitments to Asia.[42] The US also aims at safeguarding interests of its Asian allies including the management of territorial disputes such as the unresolved issues between China and other Asian states. In the aftermath of World War-II, the US remained the most dominant actor in the international system.[43] It dominated the blue waters and the skies of the Asia-Pacific including supremacy in the Indian Ocean Region (IOR) during the Cold War period. Thus, the US aims at safeguarding all the sea lines of communications that are pivotal to its economy from Asia-Pacific to the IOR.[44] On the other hand, China's size, its continental power potential[45] (a state that enjoys secure land borders in absence of serious local enemies) and growing wealth is not only building infrastructure but also building regional economic connectivity in this region. Smaller size economies of East and Southeast Asia in turn heavily rely on rising China for their future growth. The US in turn is pursuing a policy of selective engagement[46] to project its national interests[47] with states bilaterally and through regional institutions.[48] The former Defence Secretary Ash Carter highlighted that the Asia-Pacific security set-up [is] a network of bilateral, trilateral and multilateral linkages in which the US alliance system is decisively entangled.[49] Significantly, the Quadrilateral Security Dialogue (the Quad) is an informal strategic forum of the US, Australia, Japan and India. Officially, the Quad does not have an explicit target, but it is clear that it aims at outweighing China's growing influence.[50] Through such alliance system, the US maintains a consistent footprints and military force in the region thereby introducing military reforms and modernization plans, adopting new operational concepts and capabilities to changing character of warfare that in turn creates a vicious cycle of arms competition among regional states. The section below determines how the US growing military potential dominates China.

US force modernization – unfading footprints in Asia

The US preserves stockpile of 3,800 nuclear warheads, 1,930 of which are retained in deployed form (1,750 are strategic whereas 150 are non-strategic warheads). Around 2,050 are reported to be held in reserves whereas 2,650 warheads are told to be scheduled for dismantlement for a total record of 6,450 weapons.[51] The US plans on spending $700 billion to improve deterrent force over the next 25 years.[52] It aims at capitalizing $400 billion (2017–2026)[53] on its deterrent force and modernization of platforms to encounter 21st century challenges.

On land-based ballistic missiles, the US retains 441 deployed operational Minuteman III ICBMs whereas additional 249 are kept in storage.[54] The US is developing a latest class of the ICBM called Ground-Based Strategic Deterrent. On ballistic missile submarines, the US navy preserves at least 14 nuclear-powered ballistic missile submarines (SSBNs) of Ohio class, out of which 8 are stationed in the Pacific while other 6 in the Atlantic, equipped with Trident II (D5) SLBMs. Nearly 12 new SSBNs lead to replace 14 Ohio-class SSBNs due to their better efficiency in refuelling process. The US is replacing its Trident II D5 missiles with D5LE equipped with new guidance system designed to enhance flexibility to support new missions with more accuracy.[55] More so, the US possesses 500 tactical B61 bombs of all versions in its stockpile,[56] 180 of which are deployed at six diverse locations in the EU that will be replaced with modern and efficient B61-12 guided nuclear gravity bombs. Currently, the US possesses 169 heavy bombers (62 B-1Bs, 20 B-2As and 87 B-52 Hs) out of which (18 B2s and 42 B52Hs) are thought to be specified for nuclear role.[57] The US is of the intention to acquire 220 next-generation long-range nuclear bombers (including B-21) by 2040.[58] Latest Long-Range Standoff Missile that is capable of integration in B-2, B-52H and B-21 is being secured worth US $25 billion for 1,000 missiles.

Currently, the US aims to deploy ready military force to contain China's growing influence in the East and South China Seas. The US has stationed its forces, submarines and bombers in the Asia-Pacific region.[59] The US missiles defence comprised of land-based midcourse defence platforms stationed in Alaska and California, directed to counter a limited ballistic missile attack originating from Iran or North Korea. Notably, Japan and Taiwan both have acquire PAC-3 missiles defence systems. The US and South Korea are installing THAAD on South Korean territory against the North Koreans. The US at present has 28,500 military personnel, stationed in the territory of South Korea. Additionally, US multiple squadrons of F-16 units and A-10 ground attack aircrafts are stationed in South Korea.[60] There are nearly 50,000 US' troops deployed in Japan.[61] The US Conventional Prompt Global Strikes are capable of downing or disabling the A2/AD capabilities of adversaries. The US and Japan are collectively developing Aegis BMD and SM-3 Block-IIA interceptors against incoming medium- and intermediate-range missiles. The US is also purchasing cyber weapon for deterrent effect and offensive cyber war capabilities. The platforms that are a part of general modernization efforts,[62] include the fifth-generation F-35 fighter with enhanced capability, latest stealthy and long-range attack aircraft and the KC-46A new-generation tankers and cargo jets to enable proficient, and fast-track long-range positioning.[63] The US is building its dominance in space, cyber space, new technologies and it commits to nuclear retaliation in response to cyberattack as is declared in its 2018 announcements.[64]

Where does China stand?

China has achieved the status of second largest global economy thereby minimizing the power equation with the US.[65] China considers that the US military presence in Asia creates a great threat to Chinese security[66] and that the US contributes to intensification of the tension between Taiwan and China. More so, China's socio-economic growth is increasingly dependent on sea trade – especially for energy imports. Nearly 89 per cent of China's hydrocarbons are shipped through waterways.[67] Maritime transport in the IOR is limited to the smaller choke points such as Strait of Hormuz and the Strait of Malacca. Stake for China is first island chain. This chain flows from South Korea via Japan, Philippines and Malaysia to Indonesia. For Chinese, the US along with its Asian allies uses this first island chain as a tool to impede China's legitimacy. China believes that construction of its ports is purely defensive and commercial based on its economic connectivity under its Belt and Road Initiative (BRI).[68] Thus, China sees 'US military presence in Asia as destabilizing factor'[69] and its policy on South China Sea as 'Cold War mentality.'[70] China in turn leads to modernizing its technologies[71] in order to safeguard its economic and security goals in the region.

China's force modernization and the existing gaps between China and the US

China's latest number of nuclear warheads is 350 with a total of 272 warheads that can be delivered via land-based ballistic missiles (240), aircraft (20) and nuclear-powered submarines (48). At least 150 long-range ballistic missiles (with 190 warheads) and 90 ICBM (with 130 warheads) can hit target in the US mainland. Significantly, China is developing DF-41, the latest road mobile ICBM, which is capable of carrying multiple warheads.[72] Aircraft carriers, destroyers and nuclear-powered attack submarines and A2/AD systems are part of its maritime power projection.[73] The South China Sea now is a major point of confrontation. Nearly $5.3 trillion of maritime trade passes through this sea every year. China has developed a modern fleet of its SSBN, equipped with SLBMs.[74] China has acquired 6 Jin-Class Submarines, each with potential to carry at least 12 SLBMs. China possesses SLBMs, such as JL-2 (with range of 7,200 km) and JL-2 (with range of 9,000 km). China is working on latest SSBN that is 096 Type that may carry up to 24 SLBMs. China also possesses air-launched cruise missile CJ-20.[75] It is advancing air defence capabilities to contribute to offensive and defensive operations, through providing strategic warning such as air attacks, anti-air missile defence, airborne operations and strategic airlift.[76] China is also pursuing missile defence capabilities[77] and has purchased four–six Russian S-400 systems in 2018. China has tested anti-satellite capabilities against the sun orbital objects. It has tested a nuclear capable hypersonic missile delivery vehicle and also possesses extensive modern offensive cyber capabilities.

Beijing also appears to be pursuing preemptive options well before a conflict, with the aim of eroding the US hegemonic designs, free mobility and operations in the Asia-Pacific. Nevertheless, the gap between the US and China still exists. In order to maintain regional hegemony, China needs to improve maritime potential and deterrent force on the coast around the East and South China Sea. For Beckley, China is not even close to match the US military might in Asia.[78] China today lacks power potential to dominate the East Asia Coast.[79] It lacks military power to initiate surprise attack, naval blockade or strategic bombing against Taiwan due to latter's extremely sophisticated weapons systems, early warning systems and platforms provided by the US. Additionally, Japan has a lasting A2/AD capability, thus Japan can obstruct China's Sea and air domination in the East China Sea.[80] The US dominance in the East Asian region, its potential military bases and military superiority along with military preparation of other regional states can refute China Sea and air domination both in the Western or Southern parts of the South China Sea. China experiences formidable constraints and is unable to command major portions of its seas nearby.[81]

Nevertheless, China continues to close the technological gap with the US in the field of emerging technologies, such as AI, 5G and quantum computing in their competition for technological dominance. Both great powers considered these new technologies critical to their future security and prosperity for two reasons: One, these technologies are disruptive and can radically amend the landscape of economic and military competition between the US and China. Whoever gains a supremacy in this field could reap outsize benefits and even gain everlasting power. Second, while the US possesses enduring edge in some critical sectors such as semiconductor, materials and aviation, its lead over China in these frontier technologies is relatively small, if not non-existent, since scientists and engineers in both countries are roughly at the same starting point. This raises the odds that China may outrace the US in the acquisition of certain frontier technologies.

Thus, a new Cold War competition is underway that lead to minimize the avenues for cooperation and maximize the space or confrontation between these two states. Many of the measures adopted by the US are perceived by China threatening its own security thus China in turn is gradually modernizing its defence forces and improving its maritime strength while gap still exists between the two new Cold War competitors. This shows how these states' focus on new technologies has increased while their political will to pursue disarmament goals has decreased.

India's ambitious dreams

China and India rivalry goes back to Sino-Indian war of 1962, though, the two states' economic volume is rising gradually.[82] Although China has resolved many of its border conflicts with its neighbouring countries, it continues to have strategic rivalry with India which is evident with respect to deadly border clash occurred in June 2020, in the disputed Galwan Valley, an arid Himalayan area along the Line of Actual Control, the de-facto border between the two states, left 20 Indian soldiers dead[83] while China lately announced four casualties in February 2021.[84] For some, this clash was linked to India's unilateral move last year to repeal Article 370 of the Indian constitution, which had guaranteed a measure of autonomy to the disputed Jammu and Kashmir state, which also included the disputed areas in Ladakh region. Analysts believe, the latest military standoff is also a result of China's pushback against India's recent construction of infrastructure in border areas. China objected, seeing the move as a threat to its interests in the region.[85] China's economic corridor to Pakistan and Central Asia passes through Karakoram, which is close to Galwan Valley, the site of the June 15 clash. Galwan Valley is close to Aksai Chin Plateau, which is under Chinese control but claimed by India. These developments have aggravated India's security concerns against China.

The US considers India as a stabilizer against China in Asia.[86] India is using the opportunity to cultivate its relationship with the US to advance its parochial strategic broader interests and, more specifically, to create footprint in the global market to buy sensitive hi-tech system and technologies to boost its wealth and power.[87] The US is one of the world's largest arms exporters to India at present.[88] India plays hedge against China which in turn increases its reliance on force modernization and induction of new technologies.

Indian growing reliance on weapon system: Two-prong strategy

India has stockpile of 150 nuclear warheads. India possesses 70 land-based ballistic missiles having different ranges such as: Prithvi-II (350 km), Agni–I (700+ km), Agni-II (2,000+ km), Agni-III (3,200+ km), Agni-III (3,500+ km) and Agni-V (5,200+ km). India's future plans regarding deployment of said missiles give a blend of strike options against Pakistan and China. India is building SLBMs with estimated inventory of 16 (some in development process). Its SSBNs, the Arihant is capable to carry K-15 SLBM (with range of 700 km) and the Aridhaman is capable to carry K-4 SLBM (with range of 3,500 km). The K-4 SLBMs can hit targets in Pakistan, China and in the Indian Ocean. More so, the 350 km Danush missile system also belongs to a naval-based Prithvi-II which in turn gives India a rudimentary sea-based nuclear strike capability. The Indian Air Force has Mirage 2000H a (multi-role combat aircraft) capable of carrying nuclear gravity bombs. India is advancing nuclear capable sea and air-based delivery means. India's Jaguar IS/IB fighter aircrafts are the most significant part of its nuclear strike force that are directed to China and Pakistan both.[89] India is modernizing its Mirage and Jaguar fighters and procured Rafale aircrafts to gain air supremacy.

India is also working on Nirbhay subsonic land-launched cruise missile that ranges between 700 and 1,000 km and is designed for launch from land, air and sea. India is furthering sea-launched Nirbhay for Arihant submarine and may be working on air-launched version for delivery from the Su-30MK1 aircraft.[90] India is indigenizing the BMD system laced with Advanced Air Defence and Prithvi Air Defence, respectively. India has procured S-400 air defence system from Russia that is capable of engaging the short and medium-range ballistic and cruise missiles. India is moving away from the original conception of minimum deterrence, no-first-use to a war-fighting, counterforce, preemptive and disarming first strike posture against Pakistan if not China.[91]

Hedging policy and deployment of new technologies

Two India's Vikrant-class aircraft carriers (Kiev-class and INS Vikramaditya) are under development process.[92] India projects that in the backdrop of confrontation with China, it can operationalize sea denial strategies such as sea obstruction to scuttle China's energy corridor in the IOR.[93] India procured $14 billion worth weapons and technology from the US in the last decade.[94] Indo-US Defence Trade Treaty Initiative and agreements on logistics support would lead to increase operational competence and interoperability of India allowing the US aircraft and ships to land and refuel in the Indian bases. India deceptively claims that it perceives threat from China and Pakistan. India's force modernization and power projection suggests that its ambitions go beyond this region.[95] Possibility of major war between China and India may seem less acute but Indo-China power competition has led to create severe security dilemma between India and Pakistan.

Pakistan's growing asymmetry with India:
An eye on new technologies

Pakistan certainly perceives India's deterrent force modernization as offensive that lead to increase its insecurity thereby aggravating regional asymmetries. Pakistan's evolving security posture is affected by a few plausible strategic changes occurring in the South Asian region. One, Indo-US growing strategic partnership has aggravated Pakistan's security concerns. Two, India's accumulation of power and access to the global technological market through the Nuclear Suppliers Group waiver has increased regional asymmetries thereby undermining the strategic stability. Three, in March 2019, Pakistan claims to have seen a 'demonstration of anti-satellite weapons capability [by India], when a missile defence interceptor was used to destroy a satellite in a low earth orbit and creating debris in the process.'[96] Pakistan thus perceives, these developments in the backdrop of provision of high-end technologies to India by certain states sidestepping global non-proliferation rules and increasing regional imbalance.[97] Four, India's Balakot strikes[98] inside Pakistan in the wake of Pulwama crisis have led to increase conventional arms race and the two states' preparation to fight smart and short wars in the futuristic environment. Five, the suspension of communication between India and Pakistan and a lack of arms restraint arrangement makes it more difficult for the two states to moderate the security dilemma as the likelihood and number of conflict scenarios have increased while avenues for cooperation have decreased after India's revocation of its constitutional articles on Kashmir.

In the wake of evolving dangerous patterns on violations of human rights in Kashmir, Pakistan's Inter Services Public Relations believes that India may be preparing for a false-flag operation in order to initiate and deliberately escalate war.[99] Thus, Pakistan seems to be preparing for a befitting response to such future possible crises. Six, the emergence of new technologies and weapons systems, such as BMD systems, MIRVs, sea-based systems and short-range missiles, have made deterrence stability in South Asia increasingly fragile. India's recent procurement and deployment of S-400 (three regiments against Pakistan and two against China)[100] seems to aggravate further arms race in South Asia. For Pakistan, 'Russian S-400 missile system to India could destabilize the region.'[101] It seems this development may push Pakistan for production of more missiles systems in search of deterrence stability.

The Western estimates suggest that Pakistan possesses 140–150 warheads.[102] Pakistan holds six land-based ballistic missiles in its inventory and a short-range missile that is nuclear capable such as Hatf-IX (Nasr, 60–70 Km) to counter India's Cold Start Doctrine. The road mobile Hatf-II (180 km), Hatf-III (290 km) and Hatf-IV (750 km) are also the short-range ballistic missile. Pakistan also has developed a liquid-fuelled, road mobile Hatf-V (Ghauri – 1,250 km) and the two stage, road mobile Hatf-VI (Shaheen – II–1,500 km). Pakistan developed a medium-range Shaheen-III ballistic missile variant capable of carrying nuclear and conventional warheads against Indian Agni-V. This missile carries a range of 2,750 km[103] that is capable of reaching targets throughout India including Andaman and Nicobar Island.

Pakistan possesses fighter jets such as F-16 A/B and Mirage that are assigned the nuclear role. Mirage-III is developed for test flights of nuclear-equipped Ra'ad – the air-launched cruise missile. Pakistan acquired aerial refuelling capability in order to enhance a nuclear strike mission.[104] Pakistan has developed JF-17 fighters to replace aging of Mirage-V. At sea, Pakistan has established Naval Strategic Forces Command to oversight the second strike force. It is speculated that the sea-based force consists of nuclear-armed, submarine-launched cruise missiles – deployed on 'Agosta-class' submarines or on surface ship. There are two types of cruise missiles in Pakistan's inventory: the land-based Babur (Hatf-7)[105] that also is a Naval variant. Second one is the air-launched Ra'ad (Hatf-8). Pakistan lately has developed MIRVed Ababeel, a ballistic missile against the Indian BMD system and currently working on improvement of its accuracy.

Indian arsenal will keep on growing, the improvement in censors and counterforce strategies is likely to be beneficial to India whereas expensive for Pakistan. Indian technological advancement in relation to remote sensing along with early warning system created more risks as Pakistan might experience difficulties in protection of its weapons in relation to AI and computer revolution. Pakistan certainly keeps an eye on new technologies, assesses their impact on strategic stability and will invest efforts to mitigate gaps in its inventories.

Nuclear crisis instability in the Korean Peninsula

Since the end of the Korean War, the US and South Korea have sought to deter another North Korean assault across the demilitarized zones, and more lately made concerted efforts to deter lower-level provocations conducted by Pyongyang. In turn, North Korea has worked to deter the US-Republic of Korea (ROK) invasion or coercion.

During the early decades of North-South hostility, North Korea established its deterrent goals by possessing a larger conventional force that could blunt an assault, and make the US and ROK invasion costly. North Korean artillery and missiles units deployed in forward locations had the capacity to deter South Korea. Over the last three decades, North Korea has sought to increase its capability by growing its nuclear weapon program, and an array of ballistic missile that can reach all of targets in South Korea and Japan, along with continued efforts to target the US with longer range systems.

North Korean nuclear force modernization

Democratic People's Republic of Korea's (DPRK) nuclear weapons-related pronouncements indicate deterrence as a primary reason for its nuclear build up while other suggest the reasons include domestic politics and prestige.[106] It has serious security concerns as it believes that the threat from the US has compelled it to build nuclear weapons. DPRK's conventional military balance is not in its favour against South Korea. Nevertheless, to increase its deterrent posture and in part, to offset a declining conventional capability that is costly to upgrade, DPRK has pursued in earnest capabilities such as ballistic missiles, nuclear weapons and a growing cyber capability.

Current estimates suggest DPRK's nuclear arsenal at 10–16 nuclear weapons. The North Korean missile force is composed of approximately 500 short-range Scud missiles, 150–200 medium-range Nodong missiles and a short-range KN-20 while working on medium-range Musudan and intercontinental-range KN-08. All three systems are mounted on mobile launchers. DPRK has devoted considerable efforts towards the intercontinental Taepodong missile as well as a space programme to improve its long-range capability. In February 2016, North Korea succeeded in placing a satellite in orbit further demonstrating its progress on a long-range missile. Finally, work continues on a SLBM, although there is a long way from a functional SLBM, and it seems that Kim Jong Un is seriously involved in this project as several tests have been conducted to eject an SLBM from a launching tube. North Korea is also working on its cyber capabilities as its cyber force consists of 6,000 personnel.[107]

Countermeasures adopted by ROK and the US

ROK and the US have undertaken efforts to reinforce deterrence at several levels. At the strategic level, the US and ROK signed a bilateral Tailored Strategy in October 2013 that aims at countering North Korean nuclear, chemical and biological weapon threat.[108]

This strategy establishes a strategic alliance framework for tailoring deterrence against key North Korean nuclear threat scenarios and reinforces the integration of alliance capabilities to maximize their deterrent effects. Most part of the strategy is classified but press reports suggest that the possibility of preemptive strikes against North Korean targets should there be sign that nuclear use is imminent. The shared operational plans (OPLAN) 2015 contain contingency planning for prompt strikes against North Korean leadership and military facilities. The US and ROK joint exercises[109] stimulate war plans for preemptive strikes against DPRK's nuclear weapons including its mobile missile launcher, along with underground and hardened storage facilities. The exercise in 2016 implemented a preemptive strike plan 4D (detect, disrupt, destroy and defend) that is designed to hit DPRK's nuclear and chemical facilities and assets.[110]

The two states adopted a combined counter-provocation plan for combined readiness posture to immediately and decisively respond to any North Korean provocation. The US has been working on a regional BMD system that includes its chief allies in the region i.e., Australia, South Korea and Japan. Important assets in the system include Aegis-class destroyers equipped with AN/SPY-1 radar and SM-3 surface to air missiles along with ground-based interceptors such as PAC-2 and PAC-3 systems and the THAAD systems. The US navy has Aegis destroyers stationed in Japan that often float to Korean waters to navigate a pending NK missile launches. The ROK BMD system consists of its three aegis destroyers along with PAC-2 interceptors while ROK aims at purchasing PAC-3 missiles. ROK maintain KILLCHAIN capability[111] to conduct preemptive strikes on North Korean targets with conventionally armed ballistic and cruise missiles along with air strikes. China claims that these systems are being planted to target them while ROK and China are the largest trading partners thus China pressures ROK to stay out of such plans. China expressed its opposition to the THAAD deployment as it could monitor China' action.

New technologies, strategic stability and disarmament

New technologies can gain direct and indirect military significance and in some cases may undermine strategic stability.[112] Some of these technologies include AI, biotechnology,[113] quantum computing and cryptography. They also comprise categories of outer space weapons encompassing kinetic weapons, non-kinetic physical weapons such as high-powered lasers and microwaves, cyber weapons and electronic jamming and spoofing.[114] These technologies also include weapons whose features might seem to be useful to states for executing first strikes, such as conventional and nuclear hypersonic weapons, including HGVs, HCMs and stealthy strategic autonomous systems.[115] They carry potential to enable first strikes, such as persistent surveillance technologies for tracking mobile missiles, antineutrino detectors for tracking submerged SSBNs, and some aspects of counter space and cyber weapons.

The advent of new technologies has increased the complications in achieving the goal of a world free of nuclear weapons. Responding to a question how new technologies pose challenges to nuclear disarmament, Durrani replied, 'impact of new technologies is devastating. New technologies are force multipliers but also risk multipliers given the undue advantages to some but then they also entail the danger of asymmetrical responses in the short terms and catching up by others eventually.'[116] Tariq Rauf said, 'new technologies such as hypersonic delivery systems, nuclear propelled cruise missiles and UAVs, AI, offensive cyber capabilities, new types of nuclear weapons and possible space weapons, along with non-nuclear strategic weapons have the potential to destabilize the international security system and strategic stability.'[117]

The new technologies and the possibility of their convergence, by affording more intrusion, speed, precision and lethality can threaten the core security interests of many states thus introducing non-linear pathways of escalation to the strategic level. There are quite few reasons for it such as the vulnerability of nuclear system, modernization of the delivery system and transformation in the nuclear balance. New technologies are disruptive in a sense that they aim to change the status quo to their advantage once fielded in the battlefield.

For example, the hypersonic technologies[118] are set to increase dependency on nuclear weapons because of their swift delivery mechanism and it could make the existing nuclear system increasingly risky. The hypersonic weapons[119] can carry conventional as well as nuclear weapons with the speed five times more than sound. The US, Russia and China are working for developing manoeuvrable hypersonic vehicles that could probably escape the missile defences.[120] Russia has already deployed its Avangard hypersonic missile in 2019. After successful test in 2018, President Putin in his speech declared 'Avangard is invulnerable to intercept by any existing and prospective missile defence means of the potential adversary.'[121] Conspicuously, the hypersonic weapons arms race could possibly encourage the NWS to keep reliance on the nuclear weapons in order to maintain deterrence. Probably, this could lead to further inhibition in progress towards nuclear disarmament in addition to increasing risks.[122] These are dual-use and carry misinterpretation while adversary has to keep all its system on high alert which in turn can create more risk and undermine crisis stability.

The great powers (specifically the US and China) are undergoing competition in the field of hi-tech innovations such as AI, fifth-generation telecommunication network, robotics, biotechnology and quantum computing. These new technologies may alter the economic and military balance of power prompting an aggressive competition between the states and corporations with respect to their developments and application.[123] The unprecedented advances in new weapon technology resulted in a massive revolution in military warfare.[124] The same very fact is evident in the conflicts such as Nagorno-Karabakh (between Azerbaijan and Armenia) and proxy war in Libya (between Turkey and the alliance of Saudi Arabia and UAE) witnessed use of military drones. The killing of Iranian General Qasem Suleimani and others by the US indicates the increase in the use of drones.

The MTCR developed in 1980s with an intention to prevent the spread of unmanned systems that can deliver weapons of mass destruction has not stopped the proliferation of military drones. As of March 2020, at least 102 nations had acquired military drones, and around 40 possessed, or were in the process of purchasing, armed drones. Some 35 states are now believed to own drones in the largest and deadliest class of these weapons, and at least 20 non-state actors have acquired weaponized drone technologies.[125] The Trump administration approval to incorporate changes in MTCR has further worsened the situation and could probably lead to drone arms racing.[126] Russian Kalashnikov Group expressed intentions to unveil a range of automated products that function through neural networks, a speedily learning system which operates by using preset algorithm and also acquired experience.[127] Significantly, the US and China are the leading states to develop swarming drone and furthermore, taking steps to counter the swarming tactics. Experts maintain that few drones' (underdevelopment) destructive power makes it similar to nuclear weapons.[128] The US defence department released video of autonomous drones swarm robots flying over California launched by F/A-18 aircraft. The drones function like a collective organism with one distributed brain using advanced algorithm for the purpose of decision-making and adaptation to each other like a swarm in nature. The US state department is looking it as a step ahead from its adversaries and considered to be significant development with respect to future battle networks.[129]

The world is going to enter in a warfare era where weapons will have full autonomy to make decision whom to attack without human input.[130] In 2019, the UN Secretary General Antonio Guterres to a group of governmental AI experts in a meeting stated that 'machines with the power and discretion to take lives without human involvement are politically unacceptable, morally repugnant and should be prohibited by international law.'[131] Armed drones and other weapons with varying degrees of autonomy have become far more commonly used by hi-tech militaries, including the US, Russia, the United Kingdom, Israel, South Korea and China. By 2016, China tested autonomous technologies in each domain: land, air and sea. South Korea announced in December that it was planning to develop a drone swarm that could descend upon the North in the event of war. Israel already has a fully autonomous loitering munition called the Harop, which can dive-bomb radar signals without human direction and has reportedly already been used with lethal results on the battlefield. The world's most powerful nations are already at the starting blocks of a secretive and potentially deadly arms race, while regulators lag behind.[132] The advent of military AI resulted in high level of unpredictability and complexity which could generate risks much higher than those of nuclear weapons. Commercial sector seems to be outpacing military sector in this domain. There is risk of loss of human control over full autonomous technologies that can lower the threshold of conflicts thereby increasing more stability risks.

AI and machine learning in military applications risk increasing nuclear instability.[133] One reason for this is the familiar problem of entanglement between the conventional and the nuclear realms, in particular non-nuclear threats to nuclear weapons and their command, control, communications and intelligence (C3I) systems.[134] As the effectiveness of conventional weapons improves, it becomes more feasible to use them to hold nuclear assets at risk. Autonomy in conventional weapon systems is one such advanced capability, thus feeding into the increasing entanglement and, in turn, aggravating strategic instability. One concrete example would be the deployment of stealthy UAVs and the use of swarming. AI technologies will come up with new offensive threats, as AI systems can complete tasks more successfully or take advantage of vulnerabilities in other AI systems, including autonomous weapon systems. Threats might be altered by AI technologies, making attacks typically more effective, finely targeted, difficult to attribute and more likely to exploit vulnerabilities in the AI systems of the adversary. Applications of AI in the decision-support systems that deal with the use of nuclear weapons and in the tracking and targeting of an adversary's launchers will dramatically improve targeting accuracy and, probably, increase the tempo of operations. These above facts will certainly further disrupt nuclear stability.

Space-based technologies are becoming effective for the purpose of operationalization of nuclear forces, in terms of communications for C2 systems, target identification and acquisition, surveillance, intelligence gathering, guidance for delivery systems and in BMD systems. The Intelligence, Surveillance and Reconnaissance (ISR) capabilities are essential for NWS to envision an effective first strike against nuclear adversary. Space-based technologies provide the most reliable means for real time and reliable ISR data at locations where other military tools are ineffective. States temptation for increasing congregation of communication, remote sensing and navigational satellites, significantly enhance their ISR capabilities, and subsequently, its target-acquisition capacity. These technologies are cost-effective, readily available. Remote sensing satellites are capable of mapping the adversary's assets. State using ISR capabilities are advancing. Role of private entities in production of data from various overhead sensor devices including optical and multi spectral is creating risks. This creates false sense of confidence, an adversary believes that it can track all assets from space and perceives an incentive to take them out. Worryingly, there is lack of progress in developing normative instruments to regulate these developments. Proposed Prevention of an Arms Race in Space is in stalemate since many years in CD as leader in technology development countries are unwilling to discuss this issue at international forums.

Further challenge relates to cyber space where possibility of damage is not just virtual but physical also.[135] It endangers not only nuclear landscape but also covers command and control. There are risks of information theft. Adversary might get false confidence that since these are non-kinetic technologies thus not escalatory. States have incentives to use owing to the technology being more readily available and cheaper.

The use of biotechnology techniques may significantly alter the way that the world looks at biological weapons. By enabling these weapons to become more predictable, invulnerable and lethal, biotechnology may improve their deterrence capability, especially vis-à-vis NWS. Moreover, with these new capabilities there is also the problem of detecting the biological weapons programs. So, it is possible to conclude that the genetically modified biological weapons gather two desirable characteristics for weapons of mass destruction: high lethality and detection difficulty.

Preventing proliferation of such technologies and knowledge is challenging as different actor including private sector industries are involved in this process. In fact, aforementioned efforts are going to directly impact the nature of debate generated towards nuclear disarmament and are required to be part of the Nuclear Non-proliferation Treaty dialogues.

Struggle for dominance rather than stability

Changing security environment, growing asymmetries and emerging technologies create an important divide between weapon modernization and nuclear disarmament. The multilateral or bilateral cooperative mechanisms seem weakening especially in terms of creating an enabling environment for arms control or promoting discussions on nuclear disarmament. States are struggling to create dominance than engage to stabilize the global order.

The US helped built a rules-based order in form of range of formal and informal cooperative mechanisms, regimes and treaties that led to create stability between the US and Soviet Union. Later, the US has often applied overwhelming military force – and used coercion more generally – to maintain its leadership position in the unipolar world order.[136] The US concept of influence assumes that power is more sustainably exercised when tied to democratic/liberal values.[137] Presently, the US withdrawal from negotiations over the Trans-Pacific Partnership, abandoning Joint Comprehensive Plan of Action, withdrawing from the Paris Climate Accord, derogating NATO and effectively ensuring the expiration of the World Trade Organization's appellate body have created global mistrust. The US trade disputes with longstanding allies and partners and, with its squandering use of sanctions, incentivized those friends, especially in Europe, to fashion payment mechanisms that circumvent the reach of the US dollar. Both the charm of US power and its approach to promote favourable global rules-based order has been questioned globally. It is due to the fact that the US focuses on creating dominance in order to project power beyond region rather than creating stability.

Russia under Putin has become a centralized, authoritarian state and has returned as a global player, competing with the US for parity and influence. Although it is weaker than the US both economically and military, it has the ability to intervene around the globe and to thwart the US influence. Russia is also modernizing it forces to achieve parity with the US and revocation of bilateral arms control treaties has led Russia to further modernization to deal with the US influence in Europe and Asia. States' aim at this stage is domination through force modernization not strategic stability through arms control and cooperation.

China's theory of influence, combining one-party authoritarian rule and a state-run development model, enables it to provide large grants to domestic investments in frontier technologies and gives it a major advantage over the US in building infrastructure and connectivity across Asia and beyond. The more dependent it can make other countries' economies, the more it can constrain them to its own advantage. On arms control, it categorically refuses to become a part of global mechanism due to huge arms gap between China, the US and Russia. Bilaterally, China wants the US to reduce its arsenals to the level of China to get the latter involved in constructive arms control talks. However, in Asia, arms racing trends are at rise where China wants to safeguards its own interests while the US aims at maintaining its influence in Asia. So the focus is not on stability but power projection and gaining parity to hold dominance in Asia and beyond.

Conclusion

The global security environment has become less cooperative, more conflictual, destabilised and war prone. States' reliance on deterrent force modernization and new technologies has led to increase global asymmetries and instability between rival states. States failed to incorporate cooperative mechanism in their national policies while they face renewed security threats. The US withdrawal from arms control treaties has created renewed arms racing trends thereby curtailing the space for cooperative culture. These new bilateral arms racing problem between US-Russia, US-China, China-India, India-Pakistan and in Korean Peninsula demand creation of new security mechanism and fixation of the non-proliferation treaties that become more consistent to current realities. Great power competition has led to create renewed conflicts and security concerns at the global and regional level. New security concerns have increased states reliance on force modernization and new technologies. These new technologies and arms racing trends have created asymmetries and instabilities. Lack of cooperative mechanism, arms control treaties and CBMs have made the inter-state rivalries deeply intense and complex that in turn has reduced space for consensus on regional and global disarmament.

Notes

1. Dmitry (Dima) Adamsky, 'Cross-Domain Coercion: The Current Russian Art of Strategy,' *IFRI Security Studies Center,* Proliferation Papers 54 (November 2015), pp. 9–43.
2. Tomasz Smura, 'Russian Anti-Access Area Denial (A2AD) Capabilities-Implications for NATO,' *Pulaski Policy* (November 27, 2016), pp. 1–7: https://pulaski.pl/wp-content/uploads/2015/02/Pulaski_Policy_Paper_No_29_16_EN.pdf.
3. See Sten Rynning, 'Deterrence Rediscovered: NATO and Russia,' in Frans Osinga and Tim Sweijs (ed.), *Deterrence in the 21st Century— Insights from Theory and Practice* (Verlag Berlin Heidelberg: Springer, 2021), p. 29.
4. Robert S. Ross, 'Balance of Power Politics and the Rise of China: Accommodation and Balancing in East Asia,' *Security Studies,* Vol. 15, No. 3 (August 16, 2010), pp. 355–395.
5. Ramesh Thakur, 'The Collapse of the US-Russia INF Treaty Makes Arms Control a Global Priority,' *The Conversation* (August 2, 2019): https://theconversation.com/the-collapse-of-the-us-russia-inf-treaty-makes-arms-control-a-global-priority-111251.
6. See Frank G. Hoffman, *Conflict in the 21st Century: The Rise of Hybrid Wars (Arlington:* Potomac *Institute for Policy Studies, 2007).*
7. Pavel V. Konyukhovskiy and Theocharis Grigoriadis, 'Proxy Wars & the Israeli-Palestinian Conflict,' *Defence and Peace Economics,* Vol. 31, No. 8 (November 20, 2019), p. 1.
8. Christopher P Dallas-Feeney, 'Violent Non-State Actors in the Middle East: Origins and Goals,' *E-International Relations* (May 28, 2019): https://www.e-ir.info/2019/05/28/violent-non-state-actors-in-the-middle-east-origins-and-goals/.
9. Rizwana Abbasi, 'New Warfare Domains and the Deterrence Theory Crisis,' *E-International Relations* (May 13, 2020): https://www.e-ir.info/2020/05/13/new-warfare-domain-and-the-deterrence-theory-crisis/.
10. Gilford J. Ikenberry, 'From Hegemony to the Balance of Power: The Rise of China and American Grand Strategy in East Asia,' *International Journal of Korean Unification Studies,* Vol. 23, No. 2 (2014), pp. 41–63.
11. Robert Einhorn, 'Non-Proliferation Challenges Facing the Trump Administration,' *Foreign Policy at Brooking, Arms Control and Non-Proliferation Series Paper* 15 (March 2017): https://www.brookings.edu/wp-content/uploads/2017/03/acnpi_201703_nonproliferation_challenges_v2.pdf
12. Bernard Brodie (ed.), *Absolute Weapons: Atomic Power and World Order* (New York: Harcourt, Brace and Company, 1946), p. 76; and Robert J. Art, 'Between Assured Destruction and Nuclear Victory,' in Russell Hardin (ed.), *Nuclear Deterrence: Ethics and Strategy* (Chicago: University of Chicago Press, (1985), p. 127.
13. Patrick M. Morgan, *Deterrence Now* (Cambridge, Cambridge University Press, 2003), p. 8.
14. Herman Kahn, On *Escalation* Metaphor and Scenarios (New York: Praeger, 1965); and Thomas C. Schelling, *The Strategy of Conflict* (Oxford: Oxford University Press, 1960).

15. Thomas C. Schelling, 'Meteors, Mischief, and War,' *Bulletin of the Atomic Scientists*, Vol. 16, No. 7 (1960), pp. 292–300. Also see Kahn, *On Escalation*.
16. Speech of Secretary of the State, Henry A. Kissinger in Washington D.C, 'Moral Purposes and Policy Choices,' (October 8, 1973): https://history.state.gov/historicaldocuments/frus1969-76v38p1/d19.
17. Thomas C. *Schelling* and Morton H. Halperin, *Strategy and Arms Control* (New York: Twentieth Century Fund, 1961).
18. Barry Buzan, *People, States, and Fear: The National Security Problem in International Relations* (Chapel Hill: The University of Carolina Press, 1983).
19. Sameer Lalwani and Hannah (ed.), *Investigating Crises: South Asia's Lessons, Evolving Dynamics, and Trajectories* (Washington DC: Stimson Centre, 2018).
20. Michael Krepon, 'The Stability-Instability Paradox in South Asia,' *Stimson Centre* (January 1, 2005): https://www.stimson.org/2005/stability-instability-paradox-south-asia/.
21. Author's Interview with Asif Durrani
22. Ida Nygaard and Una Hakvåg, 'Why Russia Opposes a NATO Missile Defence in Europe – a Survey of Common Explanations,' *Norwegian Defence Research Establishment* (January 3, 2013), pp. 1–24: https://ffi-publikasjoner.archive.knowledgearc.net/bitstream/handle/20.500.12242/977/13-00111.pdf?sequence=1&isAllowed=y.
23. Raymond Hinnebusch, 'The US Invasion of Iraq: Explanations and Implications,' *Critique: Critical Middle Eastern Studies*, Vol. 16, No. 3 (Fall 2007), pp. 209–228.
24. Charles E. Ziegler, 'Russian–American relations: From Tsarism to Putin,' *International Politics*, Vol. 51, No. 6 (December 4, 2014), pp. 671 and 674.
25. See 'U.S. Nuclear Weapons Modernization,' *Council on Foreign Relations* (last updated on February 7, 2018): https://www.cfr.org/backgrounder/us-nuclear-weapons-modernization.
26. Nina Tennenwald, 'The Great Unraveling: The Future of the Nuclear Normative Order,' in Nina Tennenwald and James M. Acton with an introduction by Jane Vaynman (ed.), *Meeting the Challenges of New Nuclear Age: Emerging Risks and Declining Norms in the Age of Technological Innovation and Changing Nuclear Doctrines* (Cambridge: American Academy of Arts and Sciences, 2018), p. 12: https://www.researchgate.net/publication/321138392_The_Great_Unraveling_The_Future_of_the_Nuclear_Normative_Order.
27. Charles E. Zeigler, 'International Dimensions of Electoral Processes: Russia, the USA, and the 2016 Elections,' *International Politics*, Vol. 55, No. 5 (September 2018), pp. 557–574.
28. Charles E. Zeigler, 'A Crisis of Diverging Perspectives: U.S.-Russian Relations and the Security Dilemma,' *Texas National Security Review*, Vol. 4, No. 1 (Winter 2020/2021): https://tnsr.org/2020/11/a-crisis-of-diverging-perspectives-u-s-russian-relations-and-the-security-dilemma/.
29. Hans M. Kristensen & Matt Korda, 'Russian nuclear forces, 2020,' *Bulletin of the Atomic Scientists*, Vol. 76, No. 2 (2020), p. 102.

30. Ibid.
31. Ibid.
32. Ibid., 103–105.
33. Ibid., 109.
34. Ibid., 111.
35. See 'Russia's Nuclear Weapons: Doctrine, Forces, and Modernization,' *Congressional Research Service* (Updated July 20, 2020), pp. 21–22: https://fas.org/sgp/crs/nuke/R45861.pdf.
36. Ibid., p. 24.
37. See 'Russia Test-Launches Tsirkon Hypersonic Missile,' *Global Times* (November 27, 2020): https://www.globaltimes.cn/content/1208240.shtml.
38. See 'Russia's Nuclear Weapons,' p. 26.
39. Author's interview with Tariq Rauf.
40. See 'US Withdrawal from INF Treaty puts Europe (and the World) at Risk,' *The International Campaign to Abolish Nuclear Weapons*: https://www.icanw.org/us_withdrawal_from_inf_treaty_puts_europe_and_the_world_at_risk.
41. See 'IMF Survey: Asia's Importance Growing in Global Economy,' *International Monetary Fund* (May 12, 2010): https://www.imf.org/en/News/Articles/2015/09/28/04/53/socar051210a.
42. Phillip C. Saunders, 'The Rebalance to Asia: U.S.-China Relations and Regional Security,' *Strategic Forum*, No. 281 (August 2013).
43. Hassan Farooq, Muhammad Khan and Muhammad Saeed Uzzaman, 'The 21st Century World Order: Rise of China and the Challenges to American Global Hegemony,' *Asian Journal of International Peace & Security (AJIPS)*, Vol. 4, No. 2 (July–December, 2020), p. 2.
44. Being that noted, the US Western border stretches across the Pacific Ocean where the US and its allies have shared economic interests to East and Southeast Asia. For example, Japan, South Korea, Australia, Singapore, Thailand, Philippines, India, Indonesia, and Vietnam are part of this alliance system.
45. Evan Braden Montgomery, 'Competitive Strategies against Continental Power: The Geopolitics of Sino-Indian-American Relations,' *Journal of Strategic Studies*, Vol. 36, No.1 (February 5, 2013), p. 81: https://doi.org/10.1080/01402390.2012.736383.
46. Charles L. Glaser, 'A U.S.-China Grand Bargain The Hard Choice between Military Competition and Cooperation,' *International Security*, Vol. 39, No. 4 (Spring 2015), p. 54: https://doi.org/10.1162/ISEC_a_00199.
47. See Victor D. Cha, *Powerplay: The Origins of American Alliance System in Asia* (Oxford: Princeton University Press, 2016).
48. See 'The Evolving US-Asia Alliance Network,' *Center on International Cooperation* (October 26, 2016): http://cic.nyu.edu/news_commentary/evolving-us-asia-alliance-network.
49. Ibid.
50. Tsuyushi Minami, 'Will the Quad Alliance Take Off?,' *Australian Institute of International Affairs* (November 5, 2020): https://www.internationalaffairs.org.au/australianoutlook/will-the-quad-alliance-take-off/.

51. Hans M. Kristensen, 'US Nuclear Forces,' in *SIPRI Year Book 2017: Armaments, Disarmament and International Security* (SIPRI Year Book, 2018), p. 237.
52. Quoted in Brian Kalman, Edwin Watson and South Front, 'The U.S. Nuclear Deterrent Triad. Can the U.S. Afford to Modernize it?,' *Centre for Research on Globalization* (March 16, 2016).
53. Kristensen, 'US Nuclear Forces,' p. 237.
54. Ibid., p. 240.
55. Hans M. Kristensen and Robert S. Norris, 'United States Nuclear Forces,' *Bulletin of the Atomic Scientists*, Vol. 73, No. 1 (December 1, 2017), p. 52.
56. See 'The U.S. Nuclear Arsenal: A Dangerous Vestige of the Cold War,' *Union of Concerned Scientists* (February 2014), p. 3: https://www.ucsusa. org/sites/default/files/legacy/assets/documents/nwgs/nuclear-arsenal-vestige-cold-war.pdf
57. Kristensen, 'US Nuclear Forces,' p. 239–240.
58. Connie Lee, 'JUST IN: Air Force Wants to Add More Long-Range Bombers to its Inventory,' *National Defense* (April 9, 2020): https://www.nationaldefensemagazine.org/articles/2020/4/9/air-force-increases-need-for-more-longrange-bombers.
59. See 'The Asia-Pacific Maritime Security Strategy: Achieving U.S. National Security Objectives in a Changing Environment,' *Department of Defense United States of America* (July 27, 2015), pp. 19–23.
60. See 'The US has a Massive Military Presence in the Asia-Pacific. Here's What you need to know about it,' *The World* (August 11, 2017): https://www.pri.org/stories/2017-08-11/us-has-massive-military-presence-asia-pacific-heres-what-you-need-know-about-it.
61. Lara Seligman and Robbie Gramer, 'Trump asks Tokyo to Quadruple Payments for U.S. Troops in Japan,' *Foreign Policy* (November 15, 2019): https://foreignpolicy.com/2019/11/15/trump-asks-tokyo-quadruple-payments-us-troops-japan/.
62. See 'Quadrennial Defense Review 2014,' *US Department of Defense* (March, 2014), p. 36: https://archive.defense.gov/pubs/2014_Quadrennial_Defense_Review.pdf.
63. Ibid., 28.
64. Jeffrey Lewis, 'Wannacry about Trump's Nuclear Posture Review? The Global Implications od Deterring Cyber Attacks with Nuclear Weapons,' *Nuclear Threat Initiative* (June 18, 2018): https://www.nti.org/analysis/articles/wanna-cry-about-trumps-nuclear-posture-review/.
65. Hassan Farooq and Muhammad Khan, 'COVID-19: A Stimulus for Reshaping the World Order,' *Margalla Papers-2020 (Issue-II)*, p. 32
66. Zhao Tong, 'China's Strategic Environment and Doctrine,' in Robert Einhorn and W. P. S. Sidhu (ed.), *The Strategic: Linking Pakistan, India, China and the United States* (Washington DC: Brookings Institution, March 2017), p. 17.
67. Quoted in, Jan Hornat, 'The Power Triangle in the Indian Ocean: China, India and the United States,' *Cambridge Review of International Affairs*, Vol. 29, No. 2 (2016), p. 5.
68. Alek Chance, 'The Belt and Road Initiative and the Future of Globalization,' *The Diplomat* (October 31, 2017): https://thediplomat.com/2017/10/the-belt-and-road-initiative-and-the-future-of-globalization/.

69. Quoted in Kristien Bergerson, 'China's Efforts to Counter U.S. Forward Presence in the Asia Pacific,' *U.S.-China Economic and Security Review* Commission (March 15, 2016), p. 4.
70. Justyna Szczudlik, 'China's Response to United States' Asia-Pacific Strategy,' *The Polish Institute of International Affairs,* No.41 (October 2012), p. 5.
71. See Ahley J. Tellis, Alsion Szalwinski and Michael Wills (ed.), *Strategic Asia 2017–2018: Power, Ideas and Military Strategy in the Asia-Pacific* (Washington: National Bureau of Asian Research, 2017).
72. Hans M. Kristensen & Matt Korda, 'Chinese Nuclear Forces, 2020,' *Bulletin of the Atomic Scientists* 76, No. 6 (2020), pp. 443 and 448.
73. For details 'China Naval Modernization Implications for U.S. Navy Capabilities-Background and Issues for Congress,' *Congressional Research Service* (January 27, 2021): https://fas.org/sgp/crs/row/RL33153.pdf.
74. Einhorn and Sidhu (ed.), *The Strategic: Linking Pakistan, India, China and the United States*, p. 4.
75. Kristensen & Korda, 'Chinese Nuclear Forces, 2020' pp. 451–453.
76. Oriana Skylar and Michael S Chase, 'Long-Term Competition between the United States and China in Military Aviation,' *SITC Research Briefs*, Series 9 (2017), p. 2: https://escholarship.org/content/qt00p6c0v8/qt00p6c0v8.pdf.
77. Doug Tsuruoka, 'China Pursuing Missile Defenses; Indian Nukes are Main Worry,' *Asia Times* (January 19, 2018): https://asiatimes.com/2018/01/china-pursuing-missile-defenses-indian-nukes-main-worry/.
78. Michael Beckley, 'The Emerging Military Balance in East Asia How China's Neighbors can Check Chinese Naval Expansion,' *International Security*, Vol. 42, No. 2 (Fall 2017), p. 82: https://doi.org/10.1162/ISEC_a_00294.
79. Andrew Scobell and Andrew J. Nathan, 'China's Overstretched Military,' *Washington Quarterly*, Vol. 35, No.4 (Fall 2012), pp. 141–147.
80. Berkley, 'The Emerging Military Balance in East Asia,' p. 98.
81. Ibid., pp. 104–108.
82. For interesting analysis on increasing trade volume between India and China, see Minwang Lin, 'Coordination of China and India's Development under the Initiative of the "Belt and Road",' in Rong Wang and Cuiping Zhu (ed.), *Annual Report on the Development of International Relations in the Indian Ocean Region* (Berlin: Springer, 2016), pp. 53–77.
83. Muhsin Puthan Purayil and Mufsin Puthan Purayil, 'The Ladakh Crisis and India's Ontological Security,' *Global Change, Peace & Security*, Vol. 33, No. 1 (October 01, 2020), p. 1: https://doi.org/10.1080/14781158.2021.1823359.
84. See 'China admits it lost four Soldiers in 2020 India Border Clash,' *Aljazeera* (February 19, 2021): https://www.aljazeera.com/news/2021/2/19/china-admits-it-lost-four-soldiers-in-2020-india-china-clash
85. See 'Five things to know about the India-China border standoff,' *Aljazeera* (June 22, 2020): https://www.aljazeera.com/news/2020/6/22/five-things-to-know-about-the-india-china-border-standoff.
86. Lisa Curtis, 'The Triangle Dynamic in Asia: The US, India, and China,' *The Heritage Foundation* Paper No. 1017 (Washington D.C.: The Heritage Foundation, 2007), p. 1.
87. Ibid., 1–4.

88. Rajat Pandit, 'US Pips Russia as Top Arms Supplier to India,' *The Times of India* (August 13, 2014): https://timesofindia.indiatimes.com/india/us-pips-russia-as-top-arms-supplier-to-india/articleshow/40142455.cms.
89. Hans M. Kristensen and Matt Korda, 'Indian Nuclear Forces, 2020,' *Bulletin of the Atomic Scientists*, Vol. 76, No. 4 (2020), pp. 217–225.
90. Yogesh Johsi, Frank O. Donnell and Harsh V. Pant, *India's Evolving Nuclear Force and Implications for U.. Strategy in the Asia Pacific* (Carlisle: Strategic Studies Institute, 2016), pp. 3–11.
91. Christopher Clary and Vipin Narang, 'India's Counterforce Temptations: Strategic Dilemmas, Doctrine and Capabilities,' *International Security*, Vol. 43, No. 3 (Winter 2018/19), pp. 7–52. Michael Krepon, 'The Counterforce Compulsion in South Asia,' *Stimson Centre* (April 12, 2017): https://www.stimson.org/2017/counterforce-compulsion-south-asia/; Shivshankar Menon, *Choices: Inside the Making of India's Foreign Policy* (Washington D.C.: Brookings Institution Press, 2016).
92. Hornat, 'The power triangle in the Indian Ocean,' p. 8.
93. Shahank Joshi, 'Why India is Becoming Warier of China,' *Current History*, Vol. 110, No. 735 (April 2011), pp. 156–161: https://doi.org/10.1525/curh.2011.110.735.156.
94. Mohan Malik, 'Balancing Act: The China-India-US Triangle,' *World Affairs*, Vol. 179, No. 1 (2016), pp. 50–51.
95. Anonymous, Authors Interview with a high profile military officer who wished to remain anonymous (Rawalpindi, February 2019).
96. See 'Statement by Mr. Sohail Mahmood, Foreign Secretary of Pakistan at the High-Level Segment of the Conference on Disarmament,' Ministry of Foreign Affairs Government of Pakistan (February 24, 2021): http://mofa.gov.pk/statement-by-mr-sohail-mahmood-foreign-secretary-of-pakistan-at-the-high-level-segment-of-the-conference-on-disarmament-24-february-2021/.
97. Ibid.
98. See 'Indian Aircraft Violate LoC, Scramble Back After PAF's Timely Response: ISPR,' *Dawn* (February 26, 2019): https://www.dawn.com/news/1466038.
99. The author's discussions with military officials based in Pakistan. Also see quoted in, 'Pakistan will give Befitting Response if India Undertakes False-Flag Operation: PM Imran,' *Dawn* (December 21, 2019): https://www.dawn.com/news/1523532.
100. Pranab Dhal Samanta, 'Russian S-400 Triumf gives India an edge against Pakistan, China,' *The Economic Times* (July 13, 2018): https://economictimes.indiatimes.com/news/defence/russian-s-400-gives-india-an-edge-against-pakistan-china/articleshow/54893457.cms?from=mdr.
101. See 'Russia's Sale of S-400 Missiles to India may Destabilize Region,' *Dawn* (October 20, 2018): https://www.dawn.com/news/1440164.
102. Hans M. Kristensen, Robert S. Norris, and Julia Diamond, 'Pakistani Nuclear Force, 2018,' *Bulletin of Atomic Scientists*, Vol. 74, No. 5 (2018), p. 348: https://doi.org/10.1080/00963402.2018.1507796.
103. See ISPR Press Release, No PR-61/2015-ISPR (March 09, 2015): https://www.ispr.gov.pk/press-release-detail.php?id=2804.
104. Kristensen, Norris, and Diamond, 'Pakistani Nuclear Force, 2018,' p. 352.

105. See Pakistan's ISPR Press release: No PR-10/2017-ISPR, Rawalpindi (January 09, 2017): https://www.ispr.gov.pk/press-release-detail.php? id=3672.
106. Terence Roehrig, 'North Korea, Nuclear Weapons, and the Stability-Instability Paradox,' *The Korean Journal of Defense Analysis,* Vol. 28, No. 2 (June, 2016), p. 187.
107. Emma Chanlett-Avery, Liana W. Rosen, John W. Rollins and Catherine A. Theohary, 'North Korean Cyber Capabilities: In Brief,' *Congressional Research Service* (August 3, 2017), p. 2: https://fas.org/sgp/crs/row/R44912.pdf.
108. See 'North Korea,' *Nuclear Threat Initiative* (last updated on April, 2018): https://www.nti.org/learn/countries/north-korea/chemical/.
109. Evans Revere, 'The U.S.-ROK Alliance: Projecting U.S. Power and Preserving Stability in Northeast Asia,' *Brookings, Asian Alliances Working Paper Series,* Paper 3(2016): https://www.brookings.edu/wp-content/uploads/2016/07/Paper-3.pdf.
110. Bruce Klingner, 'Save Preemption for Imminent North Korean Attack,' *The Heritage Foundation*, No. 3195 (March 1, 2017), p. 6: https://www.heritage.org/sites/default/files/2017-05/BG3195.pdf.
111. Ibid., p. 6.
112. Christopher F. Chyba, 'New Technologies & Strategic Stability,' *Dædalus, Journal of the American Academy of Arts & Sciences* (Spring2020), p. 150.
113. Francisco Galamas, 'Biotechnology and Biological Weapons: Challenges to the U.S. Regional Stability Strategy,' *Comparative Strategy,* Vol. 28, No. 2 (2009), pp. 164–169.
114. Chyba, 'New Technologies & Strategic Stability,' p. 150.
115. Ibid.
116. Author's Interview with Asif Durrani.
117. Author's Interview with Tariq Rauf.
118. Amy F. Woolf, 'Conventional Prompt Glob-al Strike and Long-Range Ballistic Missiles: Background and Issues.' *Congressional Research Service* (January 8, 2019): https://apps.dtic.mil/sti/pdfs/AD1066007.pdf; James M. Acton, 'Hypersonic Boost-Glide Weapons,' *Science & Global Security,* Vol. 23, No. 3 (2015), pp. 191–219. Richard H. Speier, George Nacouzi, Car rie Lee, and Richard M. Moore, *Hypersonic Missile Nonproliferation: Hindering the Spread of a New Class of Weapons* (Santa Monica, Calif.: RAND Corporation, 2017): https://www.rand.org/content/dam/rand/pubs/research_reports/RR2100/RR2137/RAND_RR2137.pdf.
119. Dmitry Stefanovich, 'How to Address the Russian Post-INF Initiatives,' *European Leadership Network* (January 20, 2020): https://www.europeanleadershipnetwork.org/commentary/how-to-address-the-russian-post-inf-initiatives/.
120. Richard Stone, 'National Pride is at Stake. Russian, China and United States Race to Build Hypersonic Weapons,' *American Association for the Advancement of Science* (January 8, 2020): https://www.sciencemag.org/news/2020/01/national-pride-stake-russia-china-united-states-race-build-hypersonic-weapons.
121. See 'Russia Deploys Avangard Hypersonic Missile System,' *BBC* (December 27, 2019): https://www.bbc.com/news/world-europe-50927648.

122. Philips E. Ross, 'Russia, China, the U.S.: Who Will Win the Hypersonic Arms Race?,' *IEEE SPECTRUM* (November 17, 2020): https://spectrum.ieee.org/aerospace/aviation/russia-china-the-us-who-will-win-the-hypersonic-arms-race.
123. James L. Schoff and Asei Ito, 'Competing with China on Technology and Innovation,' *Carnegie Endowment for International Peace* (October 10, 2019): https://carnegieendowment.org/2019/10/10/competing-with-china-on-technology-and-innovation-pub-80010.
124. John Yoo, 'Embracing the Machines: Rationalist War and New Weapon Technologies,' *California Legal Review*, Vol. 105 (2017), p.443.
125. Agnes Callamard and James Rogers, 'We need a new International Accord to Control Drone Proliferation,' *Bulletin of the Atomic Scientists* (December 1, 2020).
126. Ibid.
127. See 'Kalashnikov Gunmaker Develops Combat Module based on Artificial Intelligence,' *TASS Russian News Agency* (July 5, 2017): https://tass.com/defense/954894.
128. See 'US, China Developing "Super Swarm" Drones with Destruction Power Equivalent to Nuclear Weapons,' *The EurAsian Times* (August 28, 2020): https://eurasiantimes.com/us-china-developing-super-swarm-drones-with-destruction-power-equivalent-to-nuclear-weapons/.
129. See 'Immediate Release Department of Defense Announces Successful Micro-Drone Demonstration,' *US Dept of Defense* (January 9, 2017): https://www.defense.gov/Newsroom/Releases/Release/Article/1044811/department-of-defense-announces-successful-micro-drone-demonstration/.
130. Billy Perrigo, 'A Global Arms Race for Killer Robots is Transforming the Battlefield,' *TIME* (April 9, 2018): https://time.com/5230567/killer-robots/.
131. See 'Autonomous Weapons that Kill must be Banned,' *UN News* (March 25, 2019): https://news.un.org/en/story/2019/03/1035381.
132. Perrigo, 'A Global Arms Race for Killer Robots,'.
133. Vincent Boulanin (ed.), *The Impact of Artificial Intelligence on Strategic Stability and Nuclear Risk* (Stockholm: SIPRI, 2019), pp. 90–97.
134. Ibid.
135. Andrew Futter, 'Cyber Threats and Nuclear weapons: New Questions for Command and Control, Security and Strategy,' *Royal United States Institute for Defense and Security Studies Occasional Paper* (2016): https://rusi.org/sites/default/files/cyber_threats_and_nuclear_combined.1.pdf.
136. Michael J. Mazarr and Ali Wyne, 'The Real US–China Competition: Competing Theories of Influence,' *The Interpreter* (January 29, 2020): https://www.lowyinstitute.org/the-interpreter/real-us-china-competition-competing-theories-influence.
137. John J. Mearsheimer, *The Great Delusion: Liberal Dreams and International Realities* (London: Yale University Press, 2018).

4 Bridging the gap

Creating a new security environment for nuclear disarmament

Introduction

The schism between the supporters of nuclear deterrence and disarmament advocates remained a common pattern since the advent of nuclear age. Despite the efforts undertaken by various stakeholders such as NWS, NNWS, including Non-Aligned Movement and civil society groups, the world still is facing the threat of nuclear weapons. The current international security environment challenges the existing norms on non-proliferation and disarmament, while aggravating instability at global and regional levels. The world is faced with the dilemma in terms of what should be prioritized in arms control and disarmament – reduction of nuclear weapons or maintenance of strategic stability.[3] For this, there is need for creation of a new security environment that fosters dialogue among states to comprehend the global security context, states' underlying security concerns, their bilateral threat perceptions and space to build a degree of trust in order to create an environment favourable to nuclear disarmament. Instead of focusing on numerical arms reduction and instantaneous elimination of nuclear weapons, an incremental approach on easing global tensions to promote security environment for nuclear disarmament could be more practical approach.

If international disarmament forums are to work properly, there must be broad-based consensus on all disarmament issues. Each nation has to perceive that its security interests are duly protected and recognized that by engaging in concrete disarmament negotiations it stands to gain more than it will lose. This is the only way to muster the necessary political will for concrete nuclear disarmament negotiations, which NWS have thus far refused to do.

DOI: 10.4324/9781003131205-4

Creating a new security environment

Andrew Futter does not see the current security environment as favourable to nuclear disarmament. He argued, 'we are moving into a risky and more uncertain global nuclear order, thus managing nuclear risks is arguably more pressing than entertaining genuine moves towards disarmament.'[4] On constructing new framework to achieve nuclear disarmament, Futter said, 'I won't say it's very likely but there is a possibility that the current technological developments lead to non-nuclear strategic weapons and non-nuclear deterrent. This might lead to nuclear disarmament based on technological reasons rather than any moral, legal or altruistic reasons. Though getting there would be very difficult.'[5]

It is imperative to improve the existing security environment in order to reduce states' incentive to possess nuclear weapons. The political leadership of NWS and NNWS should rebuild a common foundation for making a nuclear-free world. The final document of 2010 NPT Review Conference recognizes that easing of tensions in international system and strengthening of mutual trust and confidence is mandatory to the cause of nuclear disarmament.[6] The dialogue among various stake holders is necessary for the purpose of understanding the requirements and demands of various groups of states in order to bring change in their stand points and further cooperate in developing and implementing nuclear disarmament regime.[7] For this, trust-building among states in order to create a security environment that is conducive to maintenance of strategic stability on one hand and reaching consensus for development and implementation of step-by-step approach towards nuclear disarmament on the other hand is needed.

Reviving CD in line with the SSOD-I framework

The nuclear disarmament is interwoven with the international security environment. In the present global settings, the CD appears to be a vital organ of the multilateral security architecture. The primary mandate of the CD is nuclear disarmament, which cannot be pursued or accomplished in a void. It is imperative for the achievement of nuclear disarmament goal to bridge gaps between competing approaches while addressing the underlying security concerns that drive states to rely on nuclear weapons for self-defence. One of the primary stumbling blocks in the way of the effectiveness of the CD has been the differing priorities and preferences of states for individual items on the agenda of the CD, notwithstanding their interlinkages. Each state has endeavoured to promote progress on specific agenda items which are cost-free for them and sought to target the perceived military advantage of the other states. Pursuing a holistic approach to international peace and stability, through a balanced and comprehensive program of work, the CD can contribute to enhance security for all at the lowest level of armaments. Considering correlation between conventional weapon asymmetries and reliance on nuclear deterrence, the issue of balanced reduction of armed forces and conventional armaments deserves the attention of the CD as a part of its comprehensive and balanced program of work. In parallel, on bilateral and regional basis, states should focus on arms control, nuclear risks reduction, nuclear and missiles CBMs, code of conduct and norms building for the use of new technologies and resolution of disputes. Risk reduction measures should be pursued simultaneously at the global, regional and bilateral levels as a facilitating process to gradually develop confidence for bolder measures. New approaches must be considered keeping in view of the emergence of new kind of risks, especially in relation to emerging technologies and their impact on strategic stability and disarmament. The new mechanism offered below can play a lead role in plugging gaps in the existing non-proliferation regime thereby making it relevant to the 21st century realities.

However, that requires political will of the NWS for the revival of global consensus to deal with the challenges to international peace and stability, based on the principles outlined by the SSOD-I. Why SSOD-I framework becomes so relevant platform to engineer such a spirit for a renewed security environment to build consensus on the nuclear disarmament? The SSOD-I is regarded as a comprehensive global disarmament framework that laid down a roadmap of general and complete disarmament by adopting a stepwise approach while addressing the collective security concern of all stakeholders. The major objective of the SSOD-I initially was to create a new environment in international affairs, turn states away from the nuclear and conventional arms race, and obtain agreement on a global strategy for disarmament. The participant states (NWS and NNWS) as a whole consensually agreed on a comprehensive disarmament strategy, embodied in the final document[8] adopted at the session. It contained specific measures intended to strengthen the machinery dealing with disarmament within the UN system.[9] The final document emphasized that, in the adoption of disarmament measures, the right of each state to security should be kept in mind and that, at each stage of the disarmament process, 'the objective should be undiminished security at the lowest possible level of armaments and military forces.'[10]

Recommitment to the framework of SSOD-I will provide an opportunity to rebuild trust among states at all the level such as, between NWS and non-NPT nuclear possessor states, thereby creating harmony and trust with the civil society groups. Within the CD through SSOD-I framework, a range of new measures could be initiated at unilateral, bilateral and multilateral levels in order to create a security environment conducive to nuclear disarmament.

Through this platform, based on the principle of the undiminished security for all, the affiliation on nuclear disarmament can be built with governments, non-governmental organizations, the media, civil society and the general public. On CD, through the SSOD-I framework, global and regional confidence and security-building initiatives can be launched as a step-by-step approach by halting and reversing the arms race, building CBMs, managing conflicts, reducing risks, building code of conducts and new norms on use of new technologies and revising the structure of the NPT thereby making it consistent to the 21st century realities. These global and regional initiatives can lead to create a new security environment that in turn will reinforce states' trust to build a new road to nuclear disarmament.

Strategic dialogue among P-5 countries

It is high time for the NWS adopt a step-by-step approach by bringing some of these steps to logical conclusion as nuclear disarmament was accepted by these states as an obligation. The consensus document of the 2000 and 2010 NPT Review Conferences reaffirmed binding nature of the NPT Article VI which is not implemented. Therefore, in the present complex security environment, the first step relates to NWS' commitments to create new security environment which should be consistently linked with discussions on arms control and disarmament at the CD's forum.

The nature of relationships between the P-5 countries significantly impacts the patterns that prevail at the global and regional levels. Currently, how the US, China and Russia compete for power and geopolitical influence, will determine the pace of – and possibilities for – nuclear risk reduction, arms control and inter-state conflicts management. Thus P-5 countries should take responsibility to repair the global order and stabilize their multilateral negotiating platforms. For this, it is imperative that the P-5 countries pursue a strategic dialogue among their leaderships in order to understand underlying causes of conflicts that generate threats and subsequently, find a mechanism to mitigate regional asymmetries, promote nuclear restraint by adopting budgetary constraints. It is mandatory that great powers act responsibly and take all necessary initiatives to avoid direct and/or indirect political and security confrontation among themselves. For said purpose, it is essential to advance arms control, non-proliferation and disarmament goals simultaneously. No single component is adequate to meet the aims of the others. Each is a load-bearing pillar of a three-pillared building. Therefore, it is required that the P-5 states initiate a step-by-step approach to build new security environment among themselves:

Arms control

One, deterrence is stabilized through arms control mechanisms, risks reduction measures and the settlement of bilateral disputes through mediation or legal means. The efforts to create a security environment to achieve strategic stability should not impede the existing arms control and risks reduction dialogue between the US and Russia. Over the years, the US and Russia successfully negotiated arms control treaties and ensured efficient maintenance of strategic stability during the Cold War era. Since, the end of the Cold War and more specifically in the current times when the global political system is shifting towards multipolarity, the bilateral arms control mechanism between the US and Russia have witnessed severe setbacks. Recently, despite the agreement in principle to initiate the dialogue in summer of 2017, both great powers are found to be at odds on various issues and in fact, no tangible outcomes have so far been achieved such as risk reduction measures, a formal initiation of nuclear arms control negotiations or revised reduction mechanism under the hasty extension of New START in February 2021. Significantly, the US has already parted ways from Russia by pulling out from one of the major arms control deal, the INF Treaty.[11] Despite sharp differences between Washington and Moscow however, still there is space for convergence through selective engagement under the leadership of newly elected US President, Joe Biden. In this regard, talks between both countries' leaderships and efforts to reduce the differences even if regarded as insufficient are required to be undertaken. States should recommit themselves to upholding the existing norms and preserving legally binding agreements in order to reverse the negative trends that erode faith in arms control and non-proliferation measures. Regular and organized bilateral engagement between the US and Russia would be meaningful for both great powers as diplomacy clearly communicates the assessment of the regional dynamics and policy priorities and further assist in demarcating the red lines.[12]

The nuclear arms control mechanisms are feasible choice to make for the great powers that could create an environment suitable for nuclear disarmament. In this regard, some tangible steps are required to be undertaken by the NWS to put a halt on arm racing trends in order to ensure strategic stability in the international system. The US and Russia should strictly abide by the existing arms control treaties underpinning the global strategic balance and stability. Both the US and Russia currently possess the larger stockpile of nuclear arsenals, thus should bear special responsibility for reduction of these weapons leading to nuclear disarmament. They should continue to reduce drastically their respective nuclear arsenals on the principle of irreversibility and stop induction of new platforms in their inventories. The US and Russia should convince the rest of the NWS to reduce their nuclear arsenals to the 'minimum' possible level.

The US can play a role in rescuing the arms control treaties[13] such as the INF. US' Secretary, Blinken recently said, 'The United States is ready to engage Russia in strategic stability discussions on arms control and emerging security issues.'[14] Thus, it is important that the New START Treaty is preserved and a renewed INF style treaty is initiated. These treaties need to be preserved so that they can act as a catalyst to initiate bilateral arms reduction mechanism between rival states at a regional level.

Currently, new competitors, the US and China are behaving under anarchy as defensive realism suggests, without aiming at harming each other. It is due to the fact that 'China, is increasingly working within, rather than outside of, the Western order'[15] and the US has no option but to accommodate China. 'In the age of nuclear deterrence, great-power war is, thankfully, no longer a mechanism of historical change. War-driven change has been abolished as a historical process.'[16] Although the US-China relationship has evolved into one of the most complex and consequential relationships, they are moderating the security dilemma as both are working together on range of regional and global issues. For example, both jointly work on North Korean and Iranian nuclear ambitions, non-proliferation, climate change and global economic governance and mitigation of global financial crisis. Both regularly communicate, share thoughts on global governance, promote military-to-military relations in an effort to mitigate mistrust and misconceptions. Yet again to reinforce the importance of political solutions to disputes generating insecurities, the prospects of US-China understanding in the field of arms control will depend on the ability to settle South China sea issues. In the meanwhile, CBMs can be pursued to provide a conducive environment.

Since number of China's arsenal is small, thus aligning any arms control treaty to China with the aim to minimize arms racing problems and stability challenges in the Asia-Pacific is bound to fail. Rather than seeking to engage China on reductions, China might be amenable to talk about restraints and CBMs. Therefore, a stepwise approach to include China on ABMs (since it concerns Chinese also) becomes imperative. The broadening of the agenda on strategic stability related talk may offer more suitable forum for mitigating broader political differences.

Predictability and transparency

In order to prevent direct confrontations and uncontrollable escalation, the NWS should make efforts to ensure predictability and transparency by opening up all the communication channels to avert or diffuse any occurrence in air, sea and land involving their armed forces. In addition to functional communication lines, the leadership in the US, Russia and China are required to undergo regular engagement on issues related to strategic stability.[17] Secretary Blinken said, 'working with our allies and partners, the US will also demand greater transparency regarding China's provocative and dangerous weapons development programs, and continue efforts aimed at reducing the dangers posed by their nuclear arsenal.'[18] The negotiation process will assist the P-5 countries to better understand each other's positions with respect to their doctrinal changes and strategic engagements at the global and regional levels. Doctrines usually are declaratory positions and statements. However, states' security environment in practical terms is defined by the military capabilities, force postures, type and number of weapons systems deployed by their adversaries. Negotiations thus should be held to promote greater transparency in their doctrines at a practical level while moving beyond the theoretical constructs. In this way, states should minimize instabilities attached to primitive-strikes and reduce risk posed by force postures. Together with the reduction in nuclear weapons, there is a need to de-emphasize the role of nuclear weapons in military planning. The US President Biden has indicated possible review of NPR 2018 and hopefully his administration will review pursuit of tactical nuclear weapons (TNWs). Also nuclear weapons should be taken off alert and kept in de-mated form. No nuclear weapon should be allowed to be launched within minutes of notification of a missile attack. Avoiding a nuclear war by mistake is a task as important as ever. This requires attention of greater powers more than ever before.

Risk reduction measures

NWS should negotiate risk reduction measures relating to their inventories thereby commenting themselves unconditionally not to use or threaten to use nuclear weapon against NNWS or nuclear weapon-free zones, and a relevant international legal instrument should be concluded. The NWS should withdraw all the nuclear weapons deployed outside their territories and the NWS and the NNWS concerned should relinquish the nuclear umbrella and the practice of nuclear weapon sharing thereby extending negative security assurances (NSAs). On risk reduction, states should move beyond theoretical construct and focus on actual threat perceptions that force states to have reliance on nuclear capabilities. Risk reduction measures should seek a broader objective than mere management or avoidance of crisis. Their broader objective should remain the creation of an environment of trust and stability which is conducive for states to open channels of negotiations for settlement of disputes. In the absence of other measures such as settlement of long-standing disputes, there will always be potential for conflict and dangerous escalation. Disputes resolution should therefore be a fundamental element of risk reduction measures at the global, regional and bilateral level. In absence of such arrangements, sustainability of risk reduction measures will be a risk itself. Risks reduction measures need to go beyond measures for crisis stability and include steps for arms control stability. In the absence of arms control mechanism any efforts directed to risks reduction and crisis stability approved in a particular context bound to lose their practical relevance.

Elimination of tactical nuclear weapons

TNWs should clearly be included in the list of nuclear weapons considered for reductions and/or elimination. Eliminated weapons should be destroyed or dismantled. They should not be put in deposits and left ready to be used. The problem of nuclear weapons deployed in other countries' territories should be carefully considered for elimination. Only US nuclear forces are currently deployed in other countries: Belgium, Germany, Italy, the Netherlands and Turkey. Other official or de-facto nuclear powers might in the future decide to do the same, creating risky crisis situation. It is therefore, rational to refrain deployment of nuclear weapons on other countries' territories. The NATO countries should de-emphasize the role of nuclear weapons in their national security policies, military planning and strategy.

Regulate missile system and anti-ballistic missiles

The greater powers should stop the development, deployment and proliferation of advanced BMD systems and outer space weapons, which will jeopardize the nuclear disarmament process and even trigger a new round of nuclear arms race globally. There should be an agreement on restraints relating to BMD systems and cruise missiles. If the effectiveness of such systems is, as it appears, to be highly doubtful then countries should be very careful with the political and strategic implications of the deployment of such systems. There is no regime to regulate BMD systems, even The Hague code of conduct does not include BMDs. It is not worthwhile jeopardizing the reduction of nuclear weapons and the preservation of past arms control agreements, by deploying defensive systems of very dubious effectiveness.

Weaponization of outer space, threat or use of force against outer space objects, integration of ABMs with space assets and offensive doctrines and postures in outer space continue to constitute threats to space security, safety and sustainability. The convergence between space-based capabilities and military uses of emerging technologies pose new and grave dangers to security and deterrence stability. Precision systems coupled with anti-ballistic missile systems will give states a false sense of security that in turn will encourage nuclear misadventures and counter-force, preemptive strikes. There is no regime regulating these missile systems. MTCR restricts the missile but the constraints on ABM systems and cruise missiles are not covered in even The Hague code of conduct. States should clarify on transparent ground which systems they retain for conventional military purposes and which are designated for nuclear role in their inventories. These states must agree on not possessing the dual role technologies.

The issue of conventional asymmetries is neither a subject of serious work at the platform of the Convention on Certain Conventional Weapons (CCCW) or the existing treaties and conventions which have remained focused on prohibitions and restrictions from the standpoint of their humanitarian impact. The negotiations on the Arms Trade Treaty were a missed opportunity to regulate the international trade in conventional arms to ensure that it does not contribute to the military imbalance and asymmetries between regional countries. Thus, a new convention needs to be initiated to regulate conventional technologies. CD should initiate process on reduction of conventional arms asymmetries, arms control and limitation given the casual relationship between conventional asymmetries and nuclear deterrence.

New treaty to regulate newer disruptive technologies

On new technologies, Futter commented, 'new technologies are making things more complicated, we need to move towards a broader conception of risks reduction which may not necessarily be focused on promoting treaties, or formal/legal tangible binding agreements but it might be just focused on creating norms, building confidence and sharing risks assessments.'[19] Arguably, a legally binding arrangement is required between the US and Russia to regulate newer disruptive technologies – GPS systems, hypersonic machines, artificial intelligence-related machines that carry the potential to disrupt strategic stability – thereby strengthening normative framework on discouraging inclusion of such technologies in military strategies. Link with nuclear disarmament 2018 US announcement provides for nuclear response to cyberattacks. First step should to strike an agreement on not to use cyberattacks against critical infrastructure and C2 systems. The rapid development of new technologies is making it mandatory to enact international laws. The spread of new technologies to all states and/or non-state actors across the world who is the desired recipients; there is an utmost need to negotiate a mechanism to control, accountability, transparency and oversight in order to ensure international peace and security. There can be a joint or separate mechanism to oversight these emerging new technologies and/or these technologies may be considered in the broader purview of non-proliferation regime. Currently, there is no formal instrument for arms control regulations that looks over the connection between the nuclear weapons and new technologies. Fu Cong, the Director-General of the Department of Arms Control of the Ministry of the Foreign Affairs of China, stated, 'Advances in emerging technologies brings about new security challenges, and the absence of international rules in these new domains is becoming increasingly prominent.'[20] Broadly speaking, lack of arms control mechanism against new technologies hampers the cause of total elimination of nuclear weapons. Arms control mechanism assists in increasing the requisite transparency and ensures predictability with respect to the strategic doctrines and postures of the states. In the absence of such a mechanism, the states are more probably to pursue ambitious policies in the wake of these new technologies and their intersection with nuclear doctrines. Numerous studies are being conducted[21] to analyse the challenges and opportunities with respect to the incorporation of emerging technologies in arms control mechanism,[22] nevertheless the determining factors in this regard are considered to be technology, application of technology and geopolitics.[23] The debate in CD should build advance public awareness while establishing an educational base to understand new wide ranging challenges that new technologies continue to pose and create some normative and legal frameworks to regulate new technologies in order to mitigate their military shocks/impacts. The current technology holders who seek to preserve their military advantage by opposing any legally binding controls on the hostile use of the emerging technologies should recognize that, given the prevalence and pervasiveness of these technologies, it would not be possible to prevent for long their hostile uses by other states and non-state actors.

After realizing the ground highlighted above, an official dialogue process should expand from P-5 countries to the non-NPT nuclear possessor states following the regional steps. The P-5 can use their leverage over non-NPT states to build a new security environment at the regional level.

Dialogue between P-5 and non-NPT NWS

The NWS that are not signatories to the NPT (India, Israel and Pakistan) and the Democratic People's Republic of Korea should be persuaded to take appropriate steps to introduce new security environment by initiating new cooperative mechanisms at the regional level. These mechanisms should aim at persuading them to resume CBMs, manage their conflicts, reduce their reliance on nuclear weapons and the number of their weapons; sign all the possible arms control agreements compatible with their status as non-NPT members; to enforce strict control of nuclear material respecting all the relevant agreement with the IAEA. Indeed, for this to happen it would be important to work on addressing their respective security concerns. Hence there is need for parallel processes to strengthen collective security mechanism and settlement of the disputes. The following steps should be undertaken in parallel by the rival states at the regional level in order to achieve deterrent stability with ultimate aim to achieve nuclear disarmament.

South Asia

Deterrence stability in South Asia can be achieved through comprehensive negotiations, arms control mechanisms, risks reduction measures, bilateral trust-building, promoting bilateral ties in economic and cultural domains and settlement of bilateral disputes through mediation or legal means. Instead of focusing on numerical arms reduction, India and Pakistan need to adopt an incremental approach on easing bilateral tensions to promote security environment for nuclear arms control leading to build a further consensus on nuclear disarmament. On the question, how the consensus on disarmament can be created in South Asia, Kamran Akhtar said, 'willingness of the parties to engage in sincere efforts for the resolution of outstanding disputes; eschewing aggressive military postures and doctrines; agreeing on CBMs and arms control measures; even-handed approach by extra-regional powers may lead the states to a renewed consensus on disarmament.'[24] Following are the step-by-step regional approaches that may lead the two states to create an environment for nuclear disarmament:

REACHING CONSENSUS (IDENTIFYING) ON MUTUAL THREATS

Strategic rivalry between adversarial states represents clash of competing interests,[25] whereas engaging in arms control signifies recognition of mutual threats to each other's security.[26] Sustainable peace requires pursuing a common framework to stabilize the relationship, as manifested in superpower rivalry during the Cold War. In case of South Asia, reaching a common framework on requirements for a stable relationship may help both Pakistan and India to identify shared risks and explore ways to address the dangers that threaten regional peace and stability. In a scenario where one nuclear-armed state contemplates war-fighting strategies, including use of counterforce weapons against adversary's nuclear retaliatory capability and launching conventional aggression below the nuclear threshold, to escape mutual vulnerability vis-à-vis the other nuclear-armed state, the prospects for arms control and disarmament would remain low. Hence, recognizing the fact that their nuclear capabilities hold them vulnerable against each other is a pre-requisite to engage in any desirable mechanism. Nevertheless, this requires a step-by-step approach, starting with strategic dialogue between Islamabad and New Delhi. This can facilitate discussions to observe restraint on the development and deployment of new weapon systems to address risks posed by emerging technologies in an already fraught security environment. In absence of any communication, the two sides are likely to remain confronting the dilemma of interpretation and assessing each other's military capabilities on the basis of worst-case scenario analyses.

UNDERSTANDING THREAT PERCEPTIONS TO
PROMOTE NUCLEAR RESTRAINT

Both the states need to pursue a strategic dialogue between military leaderships to understand underlying causes of conflicts that generate threats and then find a mechanism to mitigate regional asymmetries and promote nuclear restraint. The two states may reiterate their recognition of nuclear deterrence as factor of stability in the region, but develop an understanding that neither the use of force is feasible nor the concept of total victory is achievable, given the dangerous escalation dynamics and consequences of the employment of nuclear weapons. Refuting strategic adventurism, war-fighting strategies and ambiguous doctrines are essential for nuclear restraint. In the February 2019 crisis, after ill-conceived air strike at Balakot, Indian Prime Minister threatened Pakistan with *'Qatal ki Raat'* (the night of murder) which could rapidly lead to escalation of conflict to nuclear level. Therefore, to enhance escalation control stability, both states may agree not to attack each other's early warning systems and avoid irresponsible and politically charged nuclear signalling. Instead of pursuing counterforce capability, there is a need to proactively address possible risks posed by emerging technologies. Kamran Akhtar suggests,[27]

The emergence of new technologies can seriously undermine deterrence stability in South Asia and lower the threshold for war. Agreed measures for transparency and arms control are therefore imperative. Yet the prospects for the same are bleak since India has clubbed itself with the technology leaders who are not willing to accept any limitations on their freedom of choices and actions in terms of weapons development and deployments. Such a situation leaves no option for the adversary to look at counter-measures.

Fundamentally, discussions should emerge on institutionalizing nuclear restraint regime which should further include: (a) effective implementation of restraints on induction of destabilizing systems such as SBMs; (b) restraint on production of further MIRVs and TNWs in the future; (c) agreements on non-deployment of nuclear-capable ballistic missile systems; (d) conclude agreements on the non-deployment of weapon systems in outer space; (e) agreement on limits on production of warheads and counting and opening up of fissile material stockpiles and (f) establishing mechanism to appreciate evolving threats such as cyberattacks and drones and signing the agreement to restraint such attacks against each other's critical facilities.

TRUST BUILDING, CRISIS MANAGEMENT AND CONFLICT RESOLUTION

This can be tailored in a manner that India's security vis-a-vis a third country is not undermined. This region has examples of bilateral agreements in the past between Pakistan and India, such as prenotification of flight testing of ballistic missiles, non-attack on nuclear installations, as well as restraint measures on deployments on building of new military posts, which are specific to India and Pakistan and do not impinge on India security interests with a thirds party. The bilateral arms control mechanism, the hotline between the Director Generals of Military Operations (DGMOs),[28] and foreign secretaries, the agreement[29] on Pre-Notification of Flight Testing of Ballistic Missiles, the agreement[30] on Reducing the Risks from Accidents Relating to Nuclear Weapons, were the major bilateral nuclear agreements under the guiding framework of the Lahore Declaration.[31] This declaration needs to be revived.

India and Pakistan need to open CBMs between the highest levels of military-to-military, political-to-political leaderships and business-to-business communities. Through Kartarpur initiative,[32] people-to-people and business–to-business contacts can be encouraged. This may serve as an active trade corridor to promote religious and cultural tourism and enhance socio-economic growth of the two states. This process may normalize the charged political tempers and institutionalize the efforts to promote peace. Riaz Khan stated, 'the two countries have to normalize relations and build mutual trust. In the past seven decades, there have been periods of hope and the two countries agreed to limited but important CBMs in the security and military field, but on the whole the relations have been marked by conflict and long periods of tension.'[33] For normalization, it is necessary to mitigate mistrust and advance cooperation in soft areas such as trade, cultural connectivity and people to people dialogues and connections. Kamran Akhtar stated, 'any CBMs which are not accompanied by parallel efforts for addressing the underlying causes of conflicts have limited utility and fail to serve the desired purpose during crises; as was recently witnessed during Pulwama crisis when the Foreign Secretaries' Hotline was never used.'[34] On the question how can restraint be imposed on arms build-up, Riaz Khan suggested, 'First requirement is normalcy in relations between Pakistan and India then they should attend to formalizing measures for risk reduction and crisis management.' Riaz Khan further said, 'under the Composite Dialogue between the two countries, which was abandoned in the aftermath of Mumbai terrorist attacks, one segment was devoted to discussion on security issues.

However, the progress under this dialogue was very slow, but it was a forum where such issues could be raised and discussed.'[35]

The Kashmir issue is the most complicated conflict, which may trigger any kind of aggression and routine border skirmishes may convert into a future limited war leading to the possibility of a nuclear exchange. Thus the ongoing developments in Kashmir in the wake of revocation of the Indian constitutional articles 370 and 35A should not hinder the progress and effectiveness of the existing agreements or future CBMs between the two rival states. There is a need to involve key stakeholders including the people of Kashmir, the UN military observers' group and the US as a mediator for the resolution of Kashmir dispute. The US role is important as it enjoys a degree of leverage and influence over both India and Pakistan due to its power projection ability in the region. US may push the implementation of the UN resolutions for a lasting solution to the Kashmir conflict. With regards to renewed consensus on disarmament, Riaz Khan believed that the 'progress towards resolution of outstanding political issues can build an environment of confidence for purposeful disarmament measures.'[36] Akhtar believes that a renewed consensus on disarmament requires India to enter into a comprehensive dialogue with Pakistan to cover dispute resolution; conventional balance and nuclear and missile restraints.[37]

NUCLEAR TRANSPARENCY AND NUCLEAR
CONFIDENCE-BUILDING MEASURES (NCBMS)

The nuclear confidence-building measures (NCBMs) have not been proven very effective in the past. These NCBMs get embroiled in the backdrop of evolving situation in Kashmir after the Indian revocation of the articles 370 and 35A on 5 August 2019. Although, Pakistan did propose India a nuclear restraint regime (NRR) in 1999[38] but India categorically refused to accept. Durrani argued, 'Pakistan has already proposed strategic restraint regime with three interlocking elements: (a) nuclear restraint; (b) conventional balance and (c) resolution of core disputes, especially Jammu and Kashmir. It's up to India to take the bait.'[39] Lack of CBMs and the absence of regional arms control arrangements[40] have curtailed space for arms restraint. This in turn has pushed regional states in South Asia towards the adoption of offensive war-fighting strategies and counter-force postures with increased arms racing problems.

Argument is that instead of linking regional security threats solely to global dynamics has not proven valuable so far. The two states may work towards adopting regional approach, offer greater transparency about each other's strategic motives, doctrinal underpinnings and nuclear arsenals.

Greater nuclear transparency in the form of CBM could help strengthen regional stability and eventually create institutional framework for them to join global endeavour on nuclear disarmament process. The New START Treaty[41] can be used as a template of nuclear arms control transparency. A more comprehensive transparency regime would involve exchange of information on deployed and non-deployed strategic systems; designating conventional or nuclear role to dual-usable delivery systems, ballistic and cruise missile, transparency on the possession of fissile missiles stockpiles and separation plans on military and civilian facilities.

Enhanced transparency is needed in nuclear doctrines deployments, developments and postures. Simultaneously, following specific measures may be considered to strengthen crisis stability: (a) effective revival of bilateral hotlines to make military-to-military communication effective; (b) promote restraints on increased readiness of arsenals and (c) avoid measures that lower down the nuclear threshold and increase crisis instability.

BILATERAL NON-PROLIFERATION AGREEMENT IN SOUTH ASIA

The nuclear-armed states in South Asia may consider signing comprehensive bilateral non-proliferation agreement including the following features: (a) establish a bilateral moratorium on the non-testing of nuclear weapons[42]; (b) work together to slow down their fissile material production; (c) initiate discussions for a bilateral agreement on a separation plan for all nuclear facilities, which would include opening up all civilian nuclear facilities to the IAEA verification and (d) link the terms of this non-proliferation agreement to membership to the Nuclear Suppliers Group for non-NPT states.[43] On universality of the NPT, Kamran Akhtar said,[44] 'realistically speaking there is no appetite for the revision of the NPT to accommodate the reality of nuclear weapon states outside the NPT. Under these circumstances the best options appear to be parallel agreed and non-discriminatory criteria for mainstreaming of the non-NPT states and commitments by the non-NPT states that are equivalent to the obligations of the NPT NWS; in return for the same rights.'

To sum up on South Asia, the above incremental approaches may construct a surface for realization of deterrence stability through arms control arrangement that in turn would create a better space for a consensus on nuclear disarmament.

Korean Peninsula

Despite the huge amount of efforts invested by the world to solve the nuclear crisis in the Korean Peninsula, the issue is yet to find a practical solution.[45] The resolution of the Korean Peninsula crisis is at the core of the faith in nuclear disarmament. Multiple initiatives are required to meet the North Korean challenge. First and foremost is to provide credible security assurances to North Korea that it will not be attacked or otherwise destabilized, including the removal of the US troops from South Korea and the end of joint US-South Korea military exercises. It is also vital to assure the verified cessation of North Korean nuclear threats. Two, space for acquisition of conventional military capabilities might be given to both North and South in order to ensure somewhat deterrence against any regional and extra-regional threats. Three, economic incentive to North Korea could be a major point responsible for the success of the negotiations specifically in context of the obligations related to North Korea's commitment to denuclearization. Apropos, North Korea's security concerns and the need for economic assistance are required to be met by the US in an acceptable way to both Pyongyang and Washington.[46] Four, the return of North Korea to NPT and ban on its missile technology demand serious attention. Since 2003, within the periods of stalemate and crisis, numerous diplomatic efforts have been initiated however failed to bring back North Korea to the fold of NPT.[47] Currently, there is need to create nuclear-weapon-free zone - including the countries of North Korea, South Korea and Japan with the US, China and Russia, thereby covering NSAs to the above-mentioned in-zone countries. North Korea would be only country to abandon its nuclear weapons and the other two countries (South Korea and Japan) will have to re-affirm their non-nuclear status under the umbrella of NPT. The US security guarantee to North Korea for no nuclear attack and no aggression and on the other hand, South Korea and Japan giving up of their nuclear umbrella, would serve the purpose of not only North Korean denuclearization but of whole the Korean Peninsula. Forceful efforts are needed to bring back North Korea to NPT, nevertheless, the broader solution to the Korean Peninsula crisis could be dealt by other means such as bilateral dialogue between the US and North Korea or the regional negotiating framework of the six-party talks.[48] Finally, the nuclear risk reduction model[49] is a significant way to initiate discussions in the Korean Peninsula. Deliberations on risk reduction measures strengthen trust-building even in the existing polarized era where the genuine disarmament endeavours have stalled.[50]

Creation of the Middle East nuclear-weapon-free zones

Creation of NWFZ and the expansion of the old ones is an important instrument to prevent the introduction of nuclear weapons in specific areas. In order to promote regional NWFZs, the P-5 should reaffirm their support for existing NWFZs and sign and ratify the relevant protocols to treaties on NWFZs if they have not already done so. The Middle East NWFZ should be constantly pursued, despite the profound challenges. The P-5 countries should initiate new dialogue on the CD, through the SSOD-I framework, thereby taking a lead to promote and generate awareness on NWFZs in the region which demand urgent attention. The step that could make disarmament alienable is NSAs so that NWS refrain from using or threatening to use nuclear weapon against NNWS.

In the Middle East many states have long called for Israel's nuclear disarmament[51] as a first step towards a broader regional security process. To promote NWFZ there requires taking account of and addressing the security concerns that lie behind the compulsion of nuclear weapon possessing states to ground their security in nuclear deterrence. Confidence-building should be inclusive, meaning that equal importance should be placed on dealing with the security concerns of other states in the region, particularly as these might motivate them to acquire nuclear weapons of their own. An initiative managing regional security and reducing risks of war can be initiated in the form of involving all regional states and covering a broad range of issues, possibly including the ongoing conflicts in Syria and Yemen, conventional arms, weapons of mass destruction, nuclear safety and security and environmental threats.

The discussion on a WMD-free zone in the Middle East could be removed from the NPT review process and be held in the CD's forum under new framework of SSOD-I. If successful, this process would still have a positive impact on the NPT over time. The five NWS could also support regional arms control by issuing unconditional NSAs to all NNWS in the region – without linking such assurances to either NPT compliance or the potential establishment of a WMD-free zone.

Multilateralizing the nuclear disarmament process

A truly meaningful oriented multilateral disarmament process will have to encompass processes that seek to address the multifarious challenges to progress on nuclear disarmament. This means a broader focus than nuclear weapons alone and multiplicity of processes and platforms which are all inter-connected and synergized within a new global consensus.

Among other things the process will also have to address crises in the Biological Weapons Convention (and Chemical Weapons Convention regimes. The UN forums debating regulations of new technologies, including the work on Lethal Autonomous Weapon Systems in the framework of the CCW, the UN General Assembly led processes on international information security etc., should have interfaces with CD. Two, multidisciplinary approaches should be adopted to include civil society, social scientists and scientists who generate awareness about consequences of war. Science advice to further develop confidence in nuclear disarmament verification techniques would be an important step forward. Three, collective security mechanism is needed to perform coordinated work in the UN system on disputes resolution. All these workstreams should flow out of a new consensus on arms control and disarmament which connects them and is guided by the SSOD-I. Information about bilateral arms control should also feed into this mechanism. Finally, a mechanism for oversight and review is needed to assess progress in various streams, to assess challenges and recommend actions to ensure finalization process.

This approach offers the realistic and practical road towards a world free of nuclear weapons, instead of pressing for a legally binding instrument to prohibit nuclear weapons at this point in a manner that deepens the gap between nuclear weapon and non-nuclear weapon states.

Conclusion

This chapter aimed at bridging the divide between competing approaches such as traditional security-centric aspects and humanitarian drive to disarmament. The chapter concludes that without serious and meaningful work in the UN system for proactive security mechanism that proves guarantees for states against arbitrary action by militarily powerful states, it will not be easy to concise sates to give up nuclear weapons. Thus the study in this chapter offer the above mechanism to create new security environment that fosters dialogue among states to comprehend the global security context, states' underlying security concerns, their bilateral threat perceptions and space to gauge a degree of trust in order to create an environment favourable to nuclear disarmament. Instead of focusing on numerical arms reduction and instantaneous elimination of nuclear weapons, this study offers an incremental approach on easing global tensions to promote new security environment for nuclear disarmament. The chapter concludes that revival of CD to negotiate nuclear disarmament as a part of comprehensive program of work which provides for simultaneous effort to address non-nuclear military asymmetries, militarization of nuclear technologies, prevention of arms race in out space by using the framework offered by the SSOD-I will assist in creation of a new security environment to build a new road to disarmament.

Notes

1. Warren Chin, 'Technology, War and the State: Past, Present and Future,' *International Affairs*, Vol. 95, No. 4 (2019), pp. 765–783. See Martin van Creveld, *Technology and War from 2000 BC to the Present* (New York: Free Press, 1989).
2. 'A Report on the UN Special Session on Disarmament,' *IAEA Bulletin*, Vol. 20, No. 4: https://www.iaea.org/sites/default/files/publications/magazines/bulletin/bull20-4/20403580206.pdf
3. Emily B. Landau and Shimon Stein, 'New US Initiative: Creating an Environment for Nuclear Disarmament (CEND),' *INSS Insight No. 1177* (June 13, 2019): https://www.inss.org.il/publication/new-us-initiative-creating-environment-nuclear-disarmament-cend/.
4. Author's Interview with Andrew Futter.
5. Ibid.
6. See 'Final Document 2010 NPT Review Conference of the Parties to the Treaty on the Non-Proliferation of Nuclear Weapons,' (New York, 2010): https://www.nonproliferation.org/wp-content/uploads/2015/04/2010_fd_part_i.pdf.
7. George Perkovich, 'Will You Listen? Dialogue on Creating the Conditions for Nuclear Disarmament,' *Carnegie Endowment for International Peace* (November 2, 2018): https://carnegieendowment.org/2018/11/02/will-you-listen-dialogue-on-creating-conditions-for-nuclear-disarmament-pub-77614.
8. See 'Final Document of the Tenth Special Session of the General Assembly,' *United Nations Digital Library*: https://digitallibrary.un.org/record/218448?ln=en.
9. See 'NAM's Proposal on Fourth Special Session on Disarmament,' *New Delhi Times* (August 11, 2016): https://www.newdelhitimes.com/nams-proposal-on-fourth-special-session-on-disarmament123/.
10. Randy J. Rydell, *Bringing Democracy to Disarmament: A Historical Perspective on the Special Sessions of the General Assembly Devoted to Disarmament* (New York: United Nations, 2016).
11. Matthew Lee, 'Russia-US hold New Strategic Talks on Arms Control,' *AP News* (January 17, 2020): https://apnews.com/article/f10391cc27617da4ada7751fb2fdc872.
12. Cyrus Newlin, Heather A. Colney, Natalia Viakhireva, and Ivan Timofeev, 'U.S.-Russia Relations at a Crossroads,' *Russian International Affairs Council* (November 1, 2020): https://russiancouncil.ru/en/activity/publications/u-s-russia-relations-at-a-crossroads/.

13. For details see GötzNeuneck, 'The Deep Crisis of Nuclear Arms Control and Disarmament: The State of Play and the Challenges,' *Journal for Peace and Nuclear Disarmament*, Vol. 2, No. 2 (2019), pp. 431–52: https://doi.org/10.1080/25751654.2019.1701796.
14. See 'Secretary Blinken: Remarks at the High-Level Segment of the Conference on Disarmament,' *UN Mission to International Organizations to Geneva* (February 22, 2021): https://geneva.usmission.gov/2021/02/22/secretary-blinken-cd/.
15. Gilford J. Ikenberry, 'The Rise of China and the Future of the West: Can the Liberal System Survive?,' *Foreign Affairs,* Vol. 87, No. 1 (January-February, 2008), pp. 23–37.
16. Ibid.
17. Dmitri Trenin, 'Strategic Stability in the Changing World,' *Carnegie Moscow Centre* (March, 2019), pp. 8–9: https://carnegieendowment.org/files/3-15_Trenin_StrategicStability.pdf.
18. See 'Secretary Blinken: Remarks at the High-Level Segment.'
19. Author's interview with Andrew Futter.
20. See 'Remarks by H.E. Mr. Fu Cong, Director-General of the Department of Arms Control of the Ministry of Foreign Affairs of China on "The Future of Arms Control and Non-Proliferation Regime" at the 2019 Moscow Non-Proliferation Conference,' *Ministry of Foreign Affairs of the People Republic of China* (November 8, 2019): https://www.fmprc.gov.cn/mfa_eng/wjdt_665385/zyjh_665391/t1714403.shtml.
21. See 'SIPRI Partners with the German Federal Foreign Office for Conference on Technology and Arms Control,' *Stockholm International Peace Research Institute* (March 18, 2019): https://www.sipri.org/news/2019/sipri-partners-german-federal-foreign-office-conference-technology-and-arms-control.
22. See, Erin D. Dumbacher, 'Limiting Cyber Warfare: Applying Arms-Control Models to an Emerging Technology,' *Nonproliferation Review*, Vol. 25, No. 3–4 (2018), pp. 203–222; James Johnson, 'Artificial Intelligence and Future Warfare: International for International Security,' *Defence and Strategic Analysis*, Vol. 35, No. 2 (April, 2019), pp. 147–169; and Heather Williams, 'Asymmetric Arms Control and Strategic Stability: Scenarios for Limiting Hypersonic Glide Vehicles,' *Journal of Strategic Studies*, Vol. 42, No. 6 (August, 2019), pp. 789–813.
23. Marc Trachtenberg, 'The Past and Future of Arms Control,' *Daedalus*, Vol. 120, No. 1 Winter, 1991), pp. 203–216: http://www.sscnet.ucla.edu/polisci/faculty/trachtenberg/cv/daedalus.pdf.
24. Author's Interview with Kamran Akhtar..
25. Andrew Kydd, 'Arms Race and Arms Control: Modeling the Hawk Perspective,' *American Journal of Political Science*, Vol. 44, No. 2 (2000), pp. 228–244.
26. Sufian Ullah, 'Arms Control in Crisis: An Assessment of Contemporary Trends,' *IPRI Journal*, Vol. 20, No. 2 (Summer 2020), p. 125.
27. Author's Interview with Kamran Akhtar.
28. See Michael Krepon (ed.), *Nuclear Risk Reduction in South Asia* (New York: Palgrave Macmillan US, 2004).

29. See 'Agreement between India and Pakistan on Pre-Notification of Flight Testing of Ballistic Missiles,' *Stimson Center* (October 24, 2012): https://www.stimson.org/agreement-between-india-and-pakistan-on-pre-notification-of-flight-tes.
30. See 'Confidence-Building and Nuclear Risk-Reduction Measures in South Asia', *Stimson Center* (June 14, 2012): https://www.stimson.org/content/confidence-building-and-nuclear-risk-reduction-measures-south-asia.
31. See 'Lahore Declaration,' *Nuclear Threat Initiative* (Last Updated on October 26, 2011): https://www.nti.org/learn/treaties-and-regimes/lahore-declaration/.
32. Tridivesh Singh Maini, 'The Kartarpur Corridor and India-Pakistan Economic Linkages,' *The Diplomat* (November 16, 2019): https://thediplomat.com/2019/11/the-kartarpur-corridor-and-india-pakistan-economic-linkages/.
33. Author's e-mail Interview with Riaz Muhammad Khan, *Former Foreign Secretary, Government of Pakistan* (December 2019).
34. Author's Interview with Kamran Akhtar.
35. Author's Interview with Riaz Muhammad Khan.
36. Ibid.
37. Author's Interview with Kamran Akhtar.
38. P.R. Chari, 'Nuclear Restraint, Risk Reduction, and the Security-Insecurity Paradox in South Asia,' in Michael Krepon (ed.), *Nuclear Risk Reduction in South Asia* (New York: Palgrave Macmillan US, 2004), p. 19.
39. Author's interview with Asif Durrani, Pakistan former Ambassador.
40. Zafar Khan, 'Balancing and Stabilizing South Asia: Challenges and Opportunities for Sustainable Peace and Stability,' *International Journal of Conflict Management*, Vol. 30, No. 5 (2019), pp. 589–614.
41. See 'New START at a Glance Fact Sheets and Briefs,' *Arms Control Association* (Last reviewed February, 2021): https://www.armscontrol.org/factsheets/NewSTART.
42. See 'Pakistan offers India moratorium on Nuclear Tests,' *The Express Tribune* (August 17, 2016): https://tribune.com.pk/story/1164259/pakistan-offers-india-moratorium-nuclear-tests.
43. Rizwana Abbasi, 'Addressing Nuclear Non-proliferation and Disarmament Challenges in South Asia,' *E-International Relations* (January 6, 2018): https://www.e-ir.info/2018/01/06/addressing-nuclear-non-proliferation-and-disarmament-challenges-in-south-asia/.
44. Author's Interview with Akhtar.
45. See 'North Korea,' *Nuclear Threat Initiative* (Last updated on October, 2020): https://www.nti.org/learn/countries/north-korea/.
46. Gloria Melina Torres Rojas, 'A Peaceful Solution to the Nuclear Tensions in the Korean Peninsula,' *Razón Crítica* 9 (2020), pp. 191–193.
47. See 'Chronology of U.S.-North Korean Nuclear and Missile Diplomacy,' *Arms Control Association* (July, 2020): https://www.armscontrol.org/factsheets/dprkchron.
48. Nobuyasu Abe, 'The NPT at Fifty: Success and Failures,' *Journal for Peace and Nuclear Disarmament*, Vol. 3, No. 2 (2020), pp. 232–233.
49. Wilfred Wan, 'Nuclear Risk Reduction A Framework Analysis,' *United Nations Institute for Disarmament Research* (June, 2019): https://unidir.org/publication/nuclear-risk-reduction-framework-analysis.

50. Sico Van Der Meer, 'Nuclear Risk Reduction: A Menu of 11 Policy Options,' *Clingendael Netherlands Institute of International Relations* (June, 2018): https://www.clingendael.org/sites/default/files/2018-06/PB_Reducing_nuclear_weapons_risks.pdf.

51. Tytti Erästö, 'The Lack of Disarmament in the Middle East: A Thorn in the Side of the NPT,' *SIPRI Insights on Peace and Security*, Vol. 2019, No. 1 (January 2019), pp. 1–7 https://www.sipri.org/sites/default/files/2019-01/sipriinsight1901.pdf.

Conclusion

Existing disarmament framework: Lack of coordination and states' security considerations

The theme of this book was to build understanding on the contemporary global security environment with an aim to create a new security environment for nuclear disarmament by bridging the divide between competing approaches such as traditional security aspects and human-centred disarmament perspectives.

Drawing on past experience, this book first tackled the complex question on how effective or ineffective is the existing disarmament framework? The study argued that the construct of broader nuclear non-proliferation regime, governing the WMDs is discriminatory and lacks rule-based criteria that led to damage the credibility and stability of the regime thereby impacting the disarmament process. The NWS and NNWS are totally divided on total elimination of nuclear weapons. The depressing truth however is that the NPT legitimizes the continuous possession of nuclear weapons by five NWS and endorses disarmament of the unarmed states which create a deep division between NWS and NNWS. The NPT Article VI only loosely demands that the NWS hold negotiations on disarmament while failed to specify the exact deadline or a verification mechanism on disarmament. This evidently overburdened NNWS for upholding their obligations to non-proliferation instead of putting emphasis on NWS for their commitments to disarmament. The parallel initiatives such as export control cartels that aimed at strengthening the NPT norms and facilitate coordination among its member states failed to achieve their goals due to lack of coordination and democratization process. The P-5 states not only influenced all the review conferences but also made their implementation hard due to their national security considerations.

The states rivalry during the Cold War kept disarmament at bay while the two superpowers remained focused on arms control and non-proliferation in order to reduce risks of war. The verification mechanisms were also limited to the two states with no multilateral involvement. The debates on disarmament being promoted by the UN-led forums were predominantly influenced by the P-5 countries. Non-aligned states and humanitarian initiatives were powerful moves that led to create the SSOD-I, which was comprehensive vision to promote non-proliferation, arms control and disarmament on the basis of equality, justice and rules-based criteria. States' rivalries, P-5 countries' influence and differences between the NWS and NNWS have marginalized the spirit of the SSOD-I. The forum beyond the SSOD-I lacked a holistic and inclusive approach to nuclear disarmament. One of the primary stumbling blocks in the way of the effectiveness of the world's only permanent multilateral disarmament treaty negotiating body, CD has been the divided preferences of states for individual items on the agenda of the CD, notwithstanding their interlinkages. Each state has endeavoured to promote progress on specific agenda items which are cost-free for them and sought to target the perceived military advantage of the other states.

The existing construct on disarmament failed to identify linkage between conventional and nuclear weapon technologies. There are some treaties such as Convention on Certain Conventional Weapons, Conventional Armed Forces in Europe, the Mine Ban Treaty, Convention on Cluster Munition and Arms Trade Treaty that are non-discriminatory and promote non-proliferation of certain types of conventional technologies covering not all but certain types of the conventional weapons/technologies. Some of the above protocols also promote stability through creating balance. Most of the treaties are promoting ban based on humanitarian ground such as Land Mine Treaty and Cluster Munitions instead of maintaining balance or strategic stability. Similarly, convention on certain conventional weapons that regulate use of certain weapons that too with a view of preventing harm to humanity. The ATT had an opportunity for provision that could have incorporated the measures similar to that of Biological Weapons Convention and Chemical Weapons Convention but they linked arms race to human security while the regional stability aspect was missing in it. The challenge is that many of the conventional technologies and lethal autonomous weapon systems are not covered in these protocols established against proliferation of conventional technologies. There are export control cartels such as Wassenaar Arrangements and the MTCR. The Wassenaar Arrangement has been established in order to contribute to the regional and international security and stability, by promoting transparency and greater responsibility in transfers of conventional arms and dual-use goods and technologies, thus preventing asymmetries and destabilizing accumulations. The MTCR aims to limit the spread of ballistic missiles and other unmanned delivery systems that could be used for chemical, biological and nuclear attacks. However, these are suppliers guided cartels that work on maximization of their own interests in disregard of states' growing capabilities that may lead to create insecurities of the other states.

All the treaties and conventions directed to promote non-proliferation of nuclear, biological and chemical weapons and nuclear disarmament lacked coordination with UN conflict resolution mechanisms. Despite strong linkages between conventional and non-conventional technologies, the states failed to introduce a multilateral mechanism to constrain conventional weapons. The existing conventional weapons-related treaties are not synthesized with CD's work on nuclear disarmament. Similarly, biological and chemical convention crisis linked to nuclear disarmament create power rivalry which marred progress in the past has resurfaced in the present time. Thus, there exists enormous gap in the existing non-proliferation architecture to limit the production and transfer of conventional delivery system, UAVs, autonomous weapons and various other lethal conventional technologies that impact the disarmament process.

Nuclear disarmament objective cannot be pursued in isolation from the real security consensus of the states in an environment where asymmetries both in the nuclear and conventional realms continue to undermine security of states. Security consensus of states can easily challenge the adopted treaties. The stalemate in the CD has therefore more to do with the security dynamics between the states outside the disarmament forums than the rules of procedures. For this, there is need to create a new security environment to build a new road to nuclear disarmament, which is discussed below.

Humanitarian approaches to disarmament: Lack of states' security considerations is widening the gaps

Further aim of this book was to identify the divide between competing approaches such as traditional security-centric aspects and humanity-centred disarmament perspectives while looking into the hurdles that marginalized the prospects for disarmament. Historic progress in the field of nuclear disarmament has been due to shared efforts of civil society movements and political forces that have relied on a delicate balance of idealism and realism. On the one hand, disarmament debate is indeed justified on humanitarian ground as nuclear weapons are catastrophic and against humanity and civilization. This notion is grounded in foundation of ethics and morality. Yet on the other hand, justification for nuclear weapons rests on its substantive practical merits in guaranteeing states' genuine national security needs.

Despite strong security-centric position held by the NWS, humanitarian activists and disarmament movements succeeded to generate awareness at the grassroots level, mobilizing civil society movements at the regional and global level and by building larger coalition with governments to promote the disarmament agenda. By drawing upon millions of people around the world, civil society groups have pushed the idea of nuclear abolition to the forefront of the international political stage. The civil society brought disarmament objectives to the attention of governments and public on issues such as banning anti-personnel landmines, cluster munitions and implementation of the NPT with respect to prohibition of nuclear tests. The joint efforts by civil society actors and the national governments assisted in finalizing the Mine Ban Treaty and Cluster Munitions Convention thereby creating the conditions that enabled the CD to bring the CTBT to conclusion. The ATT was achieved through a partnership between progressive governments and global civil society from all regions of the world, mobilized by the Control Arms Coalition. The ATT case suggests an enhanced role for the UN General Assembly in disarmament and arms control policy in the future and a greater openness on the part of the General Assembly to the participation of civil society. It suggests that civil society can influence complex human security issues.

Notwithstanding, humanitarian approaches are faced with several setbacks. The humanitarian initiative championed mainly by then ICAN, affiliated groups, and numerous governments successfully led to the conclusion of TPNW. The proponents view the TPNW's legally binding prohibition of nuclear weapons as an important contribution towards the achievement and maintenance of a world free of nuclear weapons, including the irreversible, verifiable and transparent elimination of nuclear weapons. However, the treaty leaves set of serious questions and states' security considerations unanswered thereby widening gaps between NWS and NNWs instead of mitigating them.

The first problem relates to the differing perceptions of nuclear weapons between the proponents of the humanitarian initiatives on the one hand and the nuclear possessor and nuclear umbrella states on the other. While the proponents of the humanitarian initiatives view nuclear weapons as repugnant and focus on the humanitarian consequences of any use of these weapons, the nuclear possessor states, as well as countries under extended deterrence, continue to view them as a means to ensure peace and stability. The supporters of nuclear deterrence view the approach of TPNW, which disregards the very real security considerations, as idealistic and impractical.

Two, the TPNW fails to offer any mechanism regarding the process from the prohibition to the eventual elimination of nuclear weapons. It fails to answer how the process would address the underlying security concerns that push states to rely on nuclear weapons for self-defence. It fails to offer any mechanism to ensure that any immediate prohibition on nuclear weapons on humanitarian grounds will not place any states or a group of states at a military advantage vis-à-vis other states. Three, there has hardly been any debate for an alternate system for addressing asymmetries in non-nuclear military forces, collective security mechanisms and the significance of parallel work on mechanism for settlement of outstanding regional disputes and reviving and strengthening the role of the UN therein. Four, having entered into force at a time witnessing the re-emergence of multipolar strategic competition between NWS, marked by new race for modernization of nuclear weapons and their delivery systems, it can be argued that the TPNW appears to be disconnected from the contemporary realities. Five, TPNW has been criticized as having created a parallel structure that undermines the existing consensus on disarmament, as enshrined in the NPT and could undermine the extensive safeguard provisions of the IAEA. The opponents of the TPNW view the treaty as diverting attention from other disarmament and non-proliferation initiatives, such as negotiating FMCT or ratifying the CTBT. It can, therefore, be argued that the humanitarian approach to abolition has widened the gap between the NWS and NNWS rather than bridging it.

Six, while the TPNW reaffirms the conviction that the establishment of the internationally recognized NWFZ would enhance global and, regional peace and security, strengthen the non-proliferation regime and contribute towards realizing the objective of nuclear disarmament, several proponents of the TPNW themselves have not been very steadfast in terms of demonstrating their commitment to the Middle East NWFZ. Due to political considerations their support for such a zone has never gone beyond rhetoric.

Seven, apart from the political challenges, the technical challenges related to disarmament verification are still largely unaddressed in the TPNW. The foremost technical challenge relates to the process of verification of dismantlement of the weapons. This would necessitate verification and detection mechanism that is continuously and indefinitely effective and has the confidence of the international community. Such a mechanism will have to go beyond the existing IAEA authority to ensure that nuclear weapons-related activities, not necessarily involving nuclear materials are also effectively detected and countered. The TPNW fails to offer such a mechanism.

Eight, there is no mechanism in the TPNW to deal with violations. What will be the mechanism for other parties to respond to a violation after it has been detected, and the degree to which parties face incentives to cheat in the first place? The treaty also does not provide any plan of action to dissuade states from acquiring nuclear weapons by exploiting the space generated after the disarmament of all others in order to claim itself the only nuclear weapons power. It does not consider the impact of a treaty violation on the military balance and the humanitarian catastrophes which could ensue from possible misadventures of militarily advanced states in the absence of nuclear deterrence. No mechanism is provided for widespread and effective defences or a system whereby, in the event of violation, former nuclear weapons powers would be able to quickly reconstitute countervailing deterrent or reprisal forces. Finally, TPNW, the most significant outcome of the civil society states coalition lacks representation and coordination with CD's work.

To sum up, the technical and political obstacles that confront the proponents of nuclear disarmament are multifaceted and severe. Though the entry into force of the TPNW could be considered as a step towards strengthening the international norm against nuclear weapons but it cannot bridge divide between NWS and NNWS.

Contemporary security environment: Focus on dominance in arms race and new technologies rather than stability

Further aim was to comprehend how states' reliance on modernization of deterrent force has increased while their emphasis on arms control and disarmament has decreased.

The post-Cold War era, sometimes reckoned as the unipolar world in which a dominant US-led Western coalition largely set and enforced the rules of the international order, is returning to a state of sharper and more explicit great power competition. Russia and China are actively challenging the US supremacy and alliances in Eastern Europe and East Asia. They are advancing their own vision of a new multipolar order in which the US power is diluted.

Renewed great power competition has led to create intensified conflicts and security concerns at the global and regional level. Inter-state rivalries, including US-China, US-Russia, North Korea-South Korea in East Asia, China-India and India-Pakistan continue to spark insecurity and fuel vicious cycles of armament, both within and outside of these rivalries. Resurgence of conflicts and new security threats have increased states' insecurities that in turn has compelled them into renewed arms competition thereby increasing their reliance on new technologies in order to fight smart wars.

Modernization of nuclear weapon systems, introduction of new and destabilizing weapons, like the hypersonic systems, ABMs and doctrinal innovations are generating insecurity and instability. Advancements in new technologies and threatening prospects of the militarization of cyberspace, artificial intelligence, military applications of big data analytics, quantum computing, high-powered lasers and microwaves, electronic jamming and spoofing,[1] HGVs, hypersonic HCMs, stealthy strategic autonomous systems[2] and weaponization of outer space are transforming the nature of warfare. Thus, smarter technologies seem to be changing the course of nuclear weapons in the contemporary war theatre. By reducing the price of precision and advanced manufacturing, the fourth industrial revolution is creating a new generation of smaller, smarter and cheaper weapons that challenges heavy nuclear weapon systems. The world is entering an age of mass precision.

The advent of new technologies has increased the complications in achieving the goal of a world free of nuclear weapons. The new technologies and the possibility of their convergence, by affording more intrusion, speed, precision and lethality can threaten the core security interests of many states thus introducing non-linear pathways of escalation to the strategic level. There are quite few reasons for it such as the vulnerability of nuclear system, modernization of the delivery system and transformation in the nuclear balance. New technologies are disruptive in a sense that they aim to change the status quo to their advantage once fielded in the battlefield. These arms racing trends have created dangerous risks, problems of strategic instability and disarmament crisis.

That said, the contemporary global political system seems to be challenging the relevance[3] of the western-centric non-proliferation treaties. All the existing mechanisms directed to promote arms control and disarmament are in despair. Currently, states' reliance on modernization of deterrent force has increased and emphasize on disarmament decreased. States are focused on creating dominance in arms race, space and new technologies with less focus on resolving the problems of strategic instability and disarmament crisis.

Bridging the gap: Creating new security environment for nuclear disarmament

The final aim was to offers lessons how effectively can divide between the competing approaches be bridged by creating new security environment? The argument concludes that the divide between competing approaches, such as traditional security-centric aspects and humanitarian, can only be bridged by creating new security environment.

For this, the political leadership of NWS and NNWS should rebuild a common foundation for making a nuclear-free world. As the final document of 2010 NPT Review Conference recognizes that easing of tensions in international system and strengthening of mutual trust and confidence is mandatory to the cause of nuclear disarmament.[4] The dialogue among various stakeholders is necessary for the purpose of understanding the requirements and demands of various groups of states in order to bring change in their stand points and further cooperate in developing and implementing nuclear disarmament regime.[5] For this, trust building among states in order to create a security environment that is conducive to maintenance of strategic stability on one hand and reaching consensus for development and implementation of step-by-step approach towards nuclear disarmament on the other hand is needed. The new mechanism offered below can play a lead role in bridging the divide between competing approaches.

Reviving CD in line with the SSOD-I framework

In the present global settings, the CD appears to be a vital organ of the multilateral security architecture. The primary mandate of the CD is nuclear disarmament, which cannot be pursued or accomplished in a void. It is imperative for the achievement of nuclear disarmament goal to bridge gaps between competing approaches while addressing the underlying security concerns that drive states to rely on nuclear weapons for self-defence. There is need to pursue a holistic approach to international peace and stability, through a balanced and comprehensive program of work, the CD can contribute to enhance security for all at the lowest level of armaments. Considering correlation between conventional weapon asymmetries and reliance on nuclear deterrence, the issue of balanced reduction of armed forces and conventional armaments deserves the attention of the CD as a part of its comprehensive and balanced program of work. In parallel, on bilateral and regional basis, states should focus on arms control, nuclear risks reduction, nuclear and missiles CBMs, code of conduct and norms building for the use of new technologies and resolution of disputes. Risk reduction measures should be pursued simultaneously at the global, regional and bilateral levels as a facilitating process to gradually develop confidence for bolder measures. New approaches must be considered keeping in view of the emergence of new kind of risks, especially in relation to emerging technologies and their impact on strategic stability and disarmament.

However, that will require political will of the NWS for the revival of global consensus to deal with the challenges to international peace and stability, based on the principles outlined by the SSOD-I. Recommitment to the framework of SSOD-I will provide an opportunity to rebuild trust among states at all the level such as among P-5 countries, between nuclear possessor, non-NPT states and between NWS and NNWS, thereby creating harmony and trust with the civil society groups. Within the CD through SSOD-I framework, a range of new measures could be initiated at unilateral, bilateral and multilateral levels in order to create a security environment conducive to nuclear disarmament.

Through this platform, based on the principle of the undiminished security for all, the affiliation on nuclear disarmament can be built with governments, the media, civil society and the general public. On CD, through the SSOD-I framework, global and regional confidence and security building initiatives can be launched as a step-by-step approach by halting and reversing the arms race, building CBMs, managing conflicts, reducing risks, building code of conducts and new norms on use of new technologies and revising the structure of the NPT thereby making it consistent to the 21st-century realities. These global and regional initiatives (discussed in Chapter 4) can lead to create a new security environment that in turn will reinforce states' trust to build a new road to nuclear disarmament.

Strategic dialogue among P-5 countries

It is high time that the NWS adopt a step-by-step approach by bringing some of these steps to logical conclusion as nuclear disarmament was accepted by these states as an obligation. The consensus document of the 2000 and 2010 NPT Review Conferences reaffirmed binding nature of the NPT Article VI which is not implemented. Therefore, in the present complex security environment, the first step relates to NWS' commitments to create new security environment which should be consistently linked with discussions on arms control and disarmament at the CD's forum.

It is due to the fact that the nature of relationships between the P-5 countries significantly impact the patterns that prevail at the global and regional levels. Currently, how the US, China and Russia compete for power projection will determine the pace of – and possibilities for – nuclear risk reduction, arms control and inter-state conflicts management. For this it is imperative that the P-5 countries pursue a strategic dialogue among their leaderships in order to understand underlying causes of conflicts that generate threats and subsequently, find a mechanism to mitigate regional asymmetries, promote nuclear restraint by adopting budgetary constraints. It is mandatory that great powers act responsibly and take all necessary initiatives to avoid direct and/or indirect political and security confrontation among themselves. It is essential to advance arms control, non-proliferation and disarmament goals simultaneously. No single component is adequate to meet the aims of the others. Therefore, it is required that the P-5 states initiate a step-by-step approach to build new security environment (as discussed in Chapter 4). They should not only revive but initiate new arms control mechanisms, hold dialogue on maintaining predictability and transparency, initiate risks reduction measures, sign agreements on elimination of TNWs, initiate new mechanism to regulate missile system and anti-ballistic missiles, introduce a new treaty to regulate newer disruptive technologies as discussed in Chapter 4 of this volume.

Dialogue between P-5 and non-NPT NWS

After realizing the ground highlighted above, the process should expand to include an official dialogue process from P-5 countries to the non-NPT nuclear possessor states following the regional steps as discussed in Chapter 4 of this volume. The P-5 can use their leverage over non-NPT states to build a new security environment at the regional level. For example, South Asia, Korean Peninsula and Middle East are the intense region where fog of war seems high and nuclear possessor states live outside the umbrella of the NPT.

For example, new security environment in South Asia can be achieved through reaching consensus with two rival states (India and Pakistan) on mutual threats, building their understanding threat perceptions in order to promote nuclear restraint, nuclear transparency and nuclear confidence building measures, induction of a bilateral nonproliferation agreement, comprehensive negotiations on trust building, crisis management and conflict resolution through the model presented in the preceding chapter of this volume.

Instead of focusing on numerical arms reduction, India and Pakistan need to adopt an incremental approach on easing bilateral tensions to promote security environment for nuclear arms control leading to build a further consensus on nuclear disarmament. The step-by-step regional approaches, presented in Chapter 4 may lead the two states to create an environment for nuclear disarmament.

On Korean Peninsula, first and foremost step is to provide credible security assurances to North Korea that it will not be attacked or otherwise destabilized, including the removal of the US troops from South Korea and the end of joint US-South Korea military exercises. Two, space for acquisition of conventional military capabilities might be given to both North and South in order to ensure somewhat deterrence against any regional and extra-regional threats. Three, economic incentive to North Korea could be a major way forward for the success of the negotiations specifically in context of the obligations related to North Korea's commitment to denuclearization.[6] Four, the return of North Korea to NPT and ban on its missile technology demand should be initiated through dialogue process presented in the preceding chapter. Five, the US security guarantees to North Korea for no nuclear attack and no aggression and on the other hand, South Korean and Japan giving up of their nuclear umbrella, would serve the purpose of not only North Korean denuclearization but of whole the Korean peninsula. Finally, the nuclear risk reduction model[7] is a significant way to initiate discussions in the Korean Peninsula. Deliberations on risk reduction measures strengthen trust building even in the existing polarized era where the genuine disarmament endeavours have stalled.

Creation of the Middle East nuclear-weapon-free zones

Creation of NWFZ and the expansion of the old ones is an important instrument to prevent the introduction of nuclear weapons in specific areas. In order to promote regional NWFZs, the P-5 should reaffirm their support for existing NWFZs, sign and ratify the relevant protocols to treaties on NWFZs if they have not already done so. The Middle East NWFZ should be constantly pursued, despite the profound challenges. The P-5 countries should initiate new dialogue on the CD, through the SSOD-I framework, thereby taking a lead to promote and generate awareness on NWFZs in the region which demands urgent attention. The step that could make disarmament alienable is negative security assurances so that NWS refrain from using or threatening to use nuclear weapon against NNWS.

The NWFZ goal requires taking account of and addressing the security concerns that lie behind the compulsion of nuclear weapon possessing states to ground their security in nuclear deterrence. An initiative, managing regional security and reducing risks of war can be initiated in the form of involving all regional states and covering a broad range of issues such as the ongoing conflicts in Syria and Yemen, conventional arms, WMD, nuclear safety and security and environmental threats. The discussion on a WMD-free zone in the Middle East could be removed from the NPT review process and be held in the CD's forum under new framework of SSOD-I. If successful, this process would still have a positive impact on the NPT over time. The five NWS could also support regional arms control by issuing unconditional negative security assurances to all NNWS in the region – without linking such assurances to either NPT compliance or the potential establishment of a WMD-free zone.

Multilateralizing the nuclear disarmament process

A truly meaningful oriented multilateral disarmament process will have to encompass processes that seek to address the multifarious challenges to progress on nuclear disarmament. This means a broader focus than nuclear weapons alone and multiplicity of processes and platforms which are all inter-connected and synergized within a new global consensus.

Among other things, the process will also have to address crises in the BWC and CWC regimes. The UN forums debating regulations of new technologies, including the work on LAWS in the framework of the CCW, the UN General Assembly led processes on international information security etc., should have interfaces with CD. Two, multidisciplinary approaches should be adopted to include civil society, social scientists and scientists who generate awareness about consequences of war. Science advice to further develop confidence in nuclear disarmament verification techniques would be an important step forward. Three, collective security mechanism is needed to perform coordinated work in the UN system on disputes resolution. All these work streams should flow out of a new consensus on arms control and disarmament which connects them and is guided by the SSOD-I. Information about bilateral arms control should also feed into this mechanism. Finally, a mechanism for oversight and review is needed to assess progress in various streams, to assess challenges and recommend actions to ensure finalization process.

This mechanism offers a practical road toward a world free of nuclear weapons, instead of pressing for a legally binding instrument to prohibit nuclear weapons at this point in a manner that deepens the gap between nuclear weapon and non-nuclear weapon states.

Notes

1. Christopher F. Chyba, 'New Technologies & Strategic Stability'.
2. Ibid.
3. Robert Einhorn, 'Non-Proliferation Challenges Facing the Trump Administration'.
4. See 'Final Document 2010 NPT Review Conference'.
5. George Perkovich, 'Will You Listen? Dialogue on Creating the Conditions for Nuclear Disarmament'.
6. Gloria Melina Torres Rojas, 'A Peaceful Solution to the Nuclear Tensions in the Korean Peninsula'.
7. Wilfred Wan, 'Nuclear Risk Reduction A Framework Analysis'.

Bibliography

Abbasi, Rizwana (2018) 'Addressing Nuclear Non-proliferation and Disarmament Challenges in South Asia,' *E-International Relations*, January 6: https://www.e-ir. info/2018/01/06/addressing-nuclear-non-proliferation-and-disarmament-challenges-in-south-asia/

Abbasi, Rizwana and Zafar Khan (2019) *Nuclear Deterrence in South Asia: New Technologies and Challenges to Sustainable Peace*. London and New York, NY: Routledge.

Abbasi, Rizwana (August 2, 2019) 'Creating an Environment for Nuclear Disarmament,' *E-International Relations*, August 2: https://www.e-ir.info/ 2019/08/02/creating-an-environment-for-nuclear-disarmament/

Abbasi, Rizwana (May 13, 2020) 'New Warfare Domains and the Deterrence Theory Crisis,' *E-International Relations*, May 13: https://www.e-ir.info/ 2020/05/13/new-warfare-domain-and-the-deterrence-theory-crisis/

Acton, James M. (2015) 'Hypersonic Boost-Glide Weapons,' *Science & Global Security*, 23 (3): 191–219.

Akhtar, Kamran (2020) D.G. Arms Control and Disarmament, *Ministry of Foreign Affairs Islamabad,* Interview by Author.

Art, Robert J. (1985) 'Between Assured Destruction and Nuclear Victory,' in Russell Hardin (ed.), *Nuclear Deterrence: Ethics and Strategy*. Chicago, IL: University of Chicago Press.

Barak, Eitan (2010) 'Getting the Middle East Holdouts to Join the CWC,' *Bulletin of the Atomic Scientists*, 57–62: January 2010: https://journals.sage-pub.com/doi/pdf/10.2968/066001008

Bauer, Sibylle, Paul Beijer and Mark Bromley (September, 2014) 'The Arms Trade Treaty: Challenges for the First Conference of States Parties,' *SIPRI Insight on Peace and Security* 2014/2.

Beckley, Michael (Fall 2017) 'The Emerging Military Balance in East Asia How China's Neighbors can Check Chinese Naval Expansion,' *International Security*, 42 (2): 78–119.

Blacker, Coit D. and Gloria Duffy (1984) *International Arms Control: Issues and Agreements*. Stanford, CA: Stanford University Press.

Blix, Hans (2006) *Weapons of Terror: Freeing the World of Nuclear, Biological and Chemical Arms*. Stockholm: EO GrafisKa.

Boulden, Jane, Ramesh Thakur and Thomas G. Weiss (eds.) (2009) *The United Nations and Nuclear Orders*. Tokyo, New York, NY and Paris: United Nations University Press.

Boulanin, Vincent (ed.) (2019) *The Impact of Artificial Intelligence on Strategic Stability and Nuclear Risk*. Solna: Stockholm International Peace Research Institute.

Brodie, Bernard (ed.) (1980) *The Absolute Weapon: Atomic Power and World Order*. New York, NY: Harcourt, Brace.

Buzan, Barry (1983) *People, States, and Fear: The National Security Problem in International Relations*. Chapel Hill: The University of Carolina Press.

Callamard, Agnes and James Rogers (2020) 'We need a new International Accord to Control Drone Proliferation,' *Bulletin of the Atomic Scientists*: https://thebulletin.org/2020/12/we-need-a-new-international-accord-to-control-drone-proliferation/.

Cameron, Maxwell A., Robert J. Lawson and Brain W. Tomlin (eds.) (1998) *To Walk without Fear: The Global Movement to Ban Landmines*. Toronto: Oxford University Press.

Carlson, John (2019) 'Is the NPT Still Relevant? – How to Progress the NPT's Disarmament Provisions,' *Journal for Peace and Nuclear Disarmament*, 2 (1): 97–113.

Castillo, Frank M. (1990) 'The International Physicians for the Prevention of Nuclear War: Transnational Midwife of World Peace,' *Medicine and War*, 6 (4): 250–268.

Cha, Victor D. (2016) *Powerplay: The Origins of American Alliance System in Asia*. Oxford: Princeton University Press.

Chari, P.R. (2004) 'Nuclear Restraint, Risk Reduction, and the Security-Insecurity Paradox in South Asia,' in Michael Krepon (ed.), *Nuclear Risk Reduction in South Asia*. New York, NY: Palgrave Macmillan US.

Chin, Warren (2019) 'Technology, war and the state: past, present and future,' *International Affairs*, 95 (4): 765–783.

Choubey, Deepti (2010) 'Understanding the 2010 NPT Review Conference,' *Carnegie Endowment for International Peace* https://carnegieendowment.org/2010/06/03/understanding-2010-npt-review-conference-pub-40910.

Chyba, Christopher F. (2020) 'New Technologies & Strategic Stability,' *Dædalus, Journal of the American Academy of Arts & Sciences*, 149 (2): 150–170.

Clary, Christopher and Vipin Narang (2018/19) 'India's Counterforce Temptations: Strategic Dilemmas, Doctrine and Capabilities,' *International Security*, 43 (3): 7–52.

Creveld, Martin van (1989) *Technology and War from 2000 BC to the Present*. New York, NY: Free Press.

Dalton, Toby and George Perkovich (2016) 'India's Nuclear Options and Escalation Dominance,' *Carnegie Endowment for International Peace*: https://carnegieendowment.org/2016/05/19/india-s-nuclear-options-and-escalation-dominance-pub-63609.

Dee, Megan (2017) 'Group Dynamics and Interplay in UN Disarmament Forum: In Search of Consensus,' *The Hague Journal of Diplomacy*, 12 (2–3): 158–177.

Dhanapala, Jayantha and Randy Rydell (2016) 'Multilateral Diplomacy and the NPT: An Insider's Account,' in Jayantha Dhanapala and Tariq Rauf (eds.), *Reflections on the Treaty on the Non-Proliferation of Nuclear Weapons: Review Conferences and the Future of the NPT*. Stockholm: International Peace Research Institute: 5–132.

Dumbacher, Erin D. (2018) 'Limiting Cyber Warfare: Applying Arms-Control Models to an Emerging Technology,' *Nonproliferation Review*, 25 (3–4): 203–222.

Durrani, Asif (2020) Former Ambassador, *Ministry of foreign Affairs, Pakistan*, Interview by Author.

Everts, Philip P. (1984) 'The Churches and Attitudes on Nuclear Weapons: The Case of the Netherlands,' *Bulletin of Peace Proposals*, 15 (03): 227–242.

Falk, Jim (1982) *Global Fission: The Battle over Nuclear Power*. New York, NY: Oxford University Press.

Florini, Ann M. (ed.) (2000) *The Third Force: The Rise of Transnational Civil Society*. Washington, DC: Carnegie Endowment for International Peace.

Foradori, Paolo, Giampiero Giacomello and Alessandro Pascolini (eds.) (2010) *Arms Control and Disarmament: 50 Years of Experience in Nuclear Education*. Cham: Switzerland: Palgrave MacMillan.

Ford, Christopher A. (November 2007) 'Debating Disarmament: Interpreting Article VI of the Treaty on the Non-Proliferation of Nuclear Weapons,' *Nonproliferation Review*, 14 (3): 401–428.

Futter, Andrew (2021) *University of Leicester*, Telephonic Interview by Author.

Futter, Andrew (2016) 'Cyber Threats and Nuclear weapons: New Questions for Command and Control, Security and Strategy,' *Royal United States Institute for Defense and Security Studies Occasional Paper*, 1–39: https://rusi.org/sites/default/files/cyber_threats_and_nuclear_combined.1.pdf

Galamas, Francisco (2009) 'Biotechnology and Biological Weapons: Challenges to the U.S. Regional Stability Strategy,' *Comparative Strategy*, 28 (2): 164–169.

Gibbons, Rebecca Davis (July 2018) 'The Humanitarian Turn in Nuclear Disarmament and the Treaty on the Prohibition Nuclear Weapons,' *The Nonproliferation Review*, 25 (1): 11–36.

Glaser, Charles L. (2015) 'A U.S.-China Grand Bargain The Hard Choice between Military Competition and Cooperation,' *International Security*, 39 (4): 49–90.

Goldbalt, Jozef (2000) 'The Conference on Disarmament at the Crossroads: To Revitalize or Dissolve?,' *The Nonproliferation Review*, 7 (2): 104–107.

Guthrie, Richard, John Hart and Farida Kahlau (2006) 'Chemical and Biological Warfare Developments and Arms Control,' in *SIPRI Yearbook 2006: Armaments, Disarmament and International Security*. Solna: Stockholm International Peace Research Institute.

Hamel-Green, Michael (2018) 'The Nuclear Ban Treaty and 2018 Disarmament Forums: An initial Impact Assessment,' *Journal for Peace and Nuclear Disarmament*, 1 (2): 436–463.

Hawkins, Dimity (2010) 'Now We can: Civil Society and Governments Moving toward a Ban on Nuclear Weapons,' *Disarmament Forum – UNIDIR*, (4): 39–48: http://www.pircenter.org/media/content/files/12/13859891390.pdf

Hibbs, Mark (2017) 'Eyes on the Prize: India's Pursuit of Membership in the Nuclear Suppliers Group,' *The Nonproliferation Review*, 24 (3–4): 275–296.

Hinnebusch, Raymond (2007) 'The US Invasion of Iraq: Explanations and Implications,' *Critique: Critical Middle Eastern Studies*, 16 (3): 209–228.

Hornat, Jan (2016) 'The Power Triangle in the Indian Ocean: China, India and the United States,' *Cambridge Review of International Affairs*, 29 (2): 425–443.

IAEA (1978) 'A Report on the UN Special Session on Disarmament,' *IAEA Bulletin*, 20 (4): https://www.iaea.org/sites/default/files/publications/magazines/bulletin/bull20-4/20403580206.pdf

Ikenberry, Gilford J. (2014) 'From Hegemony to the Balance of Power: The Rise of China and American Grand Strategy in East Asia,' *International Journal of Korean Unification Studies*, 23 (2): 41–63.

Ikenberry, Gilford J. (2008) 'The Rise of China and the Future of the West: Can the Liberal System Survive?,' *Foreign Affairs*, 87 (1): 23–37.

Ikenberry, Gilford J. (2005) 'Power and Liberal Order: America's Postwar World Order in Transition,' *International Relations of the Asia-Pacific*, 5 (2): 133–152.

Johnson, James (2019) 'Artificial Intelligence and Future Warfare: International for International Security,' *Defence and Strategic Analysis*, 35 (2): 147–169.

Johnson, Rebecca (2009) *Unfinished Business: the Negotiation of the CTBT and the End of Nuclear Testing*. New York, NY and Geneva: United Nations.

Johnson, Rebecca (2014) 'The United Nations and Disarmament Treatise,' *United Nations UN Chronicle*, 51 (3): 25–28. https://www.un.org/en/chronicle/article/united-nations-and-disarmament-treaties

Johnson, Rebecca (2011) 'Civil Society and the Conference on Disarmament,' *UNIDIR Resources*, 1–9. https://www.unidir.org/files/publications/pdfs/civil-society-and-the-conference-on-disarmament-360.pdf

Joshi, Shashank, (2015) 'An Evolving India Nuclear Doctrine?,' in Michael Krepon, Joshua T. White, Julia Thomson and Shane Mason (eds.), *Deterrence Instability and Nuclear Weapons in South Asia*. Washington, DC: Stimson Center: 69–94.

Joshi, Shahank (2011) 'Why India is Becoming Warier of China,' *Current History*, 110 (735): 156–161.

Joshi, Yogesh, Frank O. Donnell and Harsh V. Pant (2016) *India's Evolving Nuclear Force and Implications for U.S. Strategy in the Asia Pacific*. Carlisle: Strategic Studies Institute.

Kahn, Herman (1960) *On Escalation Metaphor and Scenarios*. New York, NY: Praeger.

Khan, Riaz Muhammad (2019) *Former Foreign Secretary, Government of Pakistan*, Interview by Author.

Khan, Zafar (2019) 'Balancing and Stabilizing South Asia: Challenges and Opportunities for Sustainable Peace and Stability,' *International Journal of Conflict Management*, 30 (5): 589–614.

Klare, Michael T. (2019) 'An "Arm Race in Speed": Hypersonic Weapons and the Changing Calculus of Battle,' *Arms Control Today*, 49 (5): 6–13.

Kmentt, Alexander (2015) 'The Development of the International Initiative on the Humanitarian Impact of Nuclear Weapons and its effect on Nuclear Weapons Debate,' *International Review of the Red Cross*, 97: 681–709.

Konyukhovskiy, Pavel V. and Theocharis Grigoriadis (November 20, 2019) 'Proxy Wars & the Israeli-Palestinian Conflict,' *Defence and Peace Economics*, 31 (8): 904–926.

Krepon, Michael (2017) 'The Counterforce Compulsion in South Asia,' *Stimson Centre*: https://www.stimson.org/2017/michael-krepons-op-ed-arms-control-wonk-counterforce-compulsion-south-asia/.

Krepon, Michael, Travis Wheeler and Shane Mason (eds.) (2016) *The Lure and Pitfalls of MIRVS: From First to the Second Nuclear Age*. Washington, DC: Stimson.

Krepon, Michael (2005) 'The Stability-Instability Paradox in South Asia,' *Stimson Centre*: https://www.stimson.org/2005/stability-instability-paradox-south-asia/.

Krepon, Michael (2005) 'The Stability-Instability Paradox in South Asia,' *Stimson Centre*: https://www.stimson.org/2005/stability-instability-paradox-south-asia/.

Krepon, Michael (ed.) (2004) *Nuclear Risk Reduction in South Asia*. New York, NY: Palgrave Macmillan US.

Kristensen, Hans M. and Matt Korda (2020) 'Russian nuclear forces, 2020,' *Bulletin of the Atomic Scientists*, 76 (2): 102–117.

Kristensen, Hans M. and Matt Korda (2020) 'Indian Nuclear Forces, 2020,' *Bulletin of the Atomic Scientists*, 76 (4): 217–225.

Kristensen, Hans M. and Matt Korda (2020) 'Chinese Nuclear Forces, 2020,' *Bulletin of the Atomic Scientists*, 76 (6): 443–457.

Kristensen, Hans M. and Robert S. Norris (2018) 'North Korean Nuclear Capabilities 2018,' *Bulletin of the Atomic Scientists*, 74 (1): 41–51.

Kristensen, Hans M. (2018) 'US Nuclear Forces,' in *SIPRI Year Book 2017: Armaments, Disarmament and International Security*. Solna: Stockholm International Peace Research Institute Year Book.

Kristensen, Hans M. Robert S. Norris and Julia Diamond (2018) 'Pakistani Nuclear Force, 2018,' *Bulletin of Atomic Scientists*, 74 (5): 348–358.

Kristensen, Hans M. and Robert S. Norris (2017) 'United States Nuclear Forces,' *Bulletin of the Atomic Scientists*, 73 (1): 48–57.

Kydd, Andrew (2000) 'Arms Race and Arms Control: Modeling the Hawk Perspective,' *American Journal of Political Science*, 44 (2): 228–244.

Lalwani Sameer and Hannah (ed.) (2018) *Investigating Crises: South Asia's Lessons, Evolving Dynamics, and Trajectories*. Washington, DC: Stimson Centre.

Landau, Emily B. and Shimon Stein (June 13, 2019) 'New US Initiative: Creating an Environment for Nuclear Disarmament (CEND),' INSS Insight No. 1177: 1–4.

Lanoszka, Alexander (2019) 'The INF Treaty: Pulling Out in Time,' *Strategic Studies Quarterly*, 13 (2): 48–67.

Lin, Minwang (2016) 'Coordination of China and India's Development under the Initiative of the "Belt and Road",' in Rong Wang and Cuiping Zhu (eds.), *Annual Report on the Development of International Relations in the Indian Ocean Region*. Berlin: Springer: 53–77.

Lodgaard, Sverre (2011) *Nuclear Disarmament and Non- Proliferation towards a Nuclear-Weapons-Free World?*. London and New York, NY: Routledge.

Malik, Mohan (2016) 'Balancing Act: The China-India-US Triangle,' *World Affairs*, 179 (1): 46–57.

Mearsheimer, John J. (2018) *The Great Delusion: Liberal Dreams and International Realities*. London: Yale University Press.

Mekata, Motoko (2018) 'How Transnational Civil Society Realized the Ban Treaty: An Interview with Beatrice Fihn,' *Journal for Peace and Nuclear Disarmament*, 1 (1): 79–92.

Menon, Shivshankar (2016) *Choices: Inside the Making of India's Foreign Policy*. Washington, DC: Brookings Institution Press.

Miller, Nicholas L. and Viping Narang (2018) 'North Korea Defied the Theoretical Odds: What can we Learn from its Successful Nuclearization,' *Texas National Security Review*, 1 (2): 58–74.

Minami, Tsuyushi (2020) 'Will the Quad Alliance Take Off?,' *Australian Institute of International Affairs:* https://www.internationalaffairs.org.au/australianoutlook/will-the-quad-alliance-take-off/.

Montgomery, Evan Braden (2013) 'Competitive Strategies against Continental Power: The Geopolitics of Sino-Indian-American Relations,' *Journal of Strategic Studies*, 36 (1): 76–100.

Morgan, Patrick M. (2003) *Deterrence Now*. Cambridge, Cambridge University Press.

Neuneck, Götz (2019) 'The Deep Crisis of Nuclear Arms Control and Disarmament: The State of Play and the Challenges,' *Journal for Peace and Nuclear Disarmament*, 2 (2): 431–52.

Nogee, Joseph L. (1963) 'Propaganda and Negotiations: The Case of the Ten-Nation Disarmament Committee,' *Journal of Conflict Resolution*, 7 (3): 510–521.

Nye Jr., Joseph S. (1989) 'Arms control after the Cold War,' *Foreign Affairs*, 68 (5): 42–64.

Nygaard, Ida and Una Hakvåg (January 3, 2013) 'Why Russia Opposes a NATO Missile Defence in Europe – a Survey of Common Explanations,' *Norwegian Defence Research Establishment*, 1–23. https://publications.ffi.no/nb/item/asset/dspace:2335/13-00111.pdf

Paul, H. Nitz (January 1976) 'Assuring Strategic Stability in an Era of Détente,' *Foreign Affairs*, 54 (2): 207–232.

Pilat, Joseph F. (2007) 'The End of the NPT Regime?,' *International Affairs*, 83 (3): 469–482.

Potter, William C. and Gaukhar Mukhatzhanova (eds.) (2010) *Forecasting Nuclear Proliferation in the 21st Century: A Comparative Perspective Volume 2*. Stanford: Stanford University Press.

Price, Richard (1998) 'Reversing the Gun Sights: Transnational Civil Society Targets Landmines,' *International Organization*, 53 (3): 613–644.

Purayil, Muhsin Puthan and Mufsin Puthan Purayil (October 01, 2020) 'The Ladakh Crisis and India's Ontological Security,' *Global Change, Peace & Security*, 33 (1): 85–91.

Rauf, Tariq (2021) Vienna based expert on nuclear governance matters, and Director of Atomic Reporters, Interview by Author.

Rauf, Tariq (2019) 'Visions of Butterflies and Unicorns as the Nuclear Disarmament Architecture Collapses: The Final Session of the Preparatory Committee for the 2020 Non-Proliferation Treaty Review Conference,' *Journal of Strategic Affairs*, 2 (2): 1–26.

Rauf, Tariq and Rebecca Johnson (1995) 'After the NPT's Indefinite Extension: The Future of the Global Nonproliferation Regime,' *Nonproliferation Review*, 3 (1): 28–42.

Rauf, Tariq (2000) 'An Unequivocal Success? Implications of the NPT Review Conference,' *Arms Control Association*: https://www.armscontrol.org/act/2000-07/features/unequivocal-success-implications-npt-review-conference.

Rauf, Tariq and Rebecca Johnson (Fall 1995) 'After the NPT's Indefinite Extension: The future of Nonproliferation Regime,' *Nonproliferation Review*, 3 (1): 28–42.

Rauf, Tariq (May 11, 2020) '25 Years after the Indefinite Extension of the Nuclear Non-Proliferation Treaty: A Field of Broken Promises and Shattered Visions,' *In Depth News* https://www.indepthnews.net/index.php/opinion/3529-25-years-after-the-indefinite-extension-of-the-nuclear-non-proliferation-treaty-a-field-of-broken-promises-and-shattered-visions.

Rauf, Tariq (2016) 'Assessing the 2015 NPT Review Conference,' in Jayantha Dhanapala and Tariq Rauf (eds.), *Reflections on the Treaty on the Non-Proliferation of Nuclear Weapons: Review Conferences and the Future of the NPT*. Solna: Stockholm International Peace Research Institute: 199–209.

Rauf, Tariq (2008) 'The 2000 NPT Review Conference,' *The Nonproliferation Review*, 7 (1): 146–161.

Revere, Evans (2016) 'The U.S.-ROK Alliance: Projecting U.S. Power and Preserving Stability in Northeast Asia,' Brookings, Asian Alliances Working Paper Series, Paper 3: 1–5.

Rice, Susan and Nancy L. Mary (March 1989) '*Beyond War: A New Perspective for Social Work,*' *Social Work*, 34 (02): 175–178.

Roberts, Brad (Summer 2019) 'On Creating the Conditions for Nuclear Disarmament: Past Lessons, Future Prospects,' *The Washington Quarterly*, 42 (2): 7–30.

Roehrig, Terence (June, 2016) 'North Korea, Nuclear Weapons, and the Stability-Instability Paradox,' *The Korean Journal of Defense Analysis*, 28 (2): 181–198.

Rojas, Gloria Melina Torres (2020) 'A Peaceful Solution to the Nuclear Tensions in the Korean Peninsula,' *Razón Crítica*, 9: 191–193.

Ross, Robert S. (August 16, 2010) 'Balance of Power Politics and the Rise of China: Accommodation and Balancing in East Asia,' *Security Studies*, 15 (3): 355–395.

Rotblat, Joseph (1985) 'The Pugwash Conferences on Science and World Affairs,' *Medicine and War*, 1 (1): 51–54.

Rydel, Randy J. (2016) 'Bringing Democracy to Disarmament A Historical Perspective on the Special Sessions of the General Assembly Devoted to Disarmament,' UNODA Occasional Paper, No. 29: 7–42.

Rydell, Randy (2007) 'Security through Disarmament: The Story of the Weapons of Mass Destruction Commission,' *The Hague Journal of Diplomacy*, 2 (1): 81–91.

Rynning, Sten (2021) 'Deterrence Rediscovered: NATO and Russia,' in Frans Osinga and Tim *Sweijs* (eds.), *Deterrence in the 21st Century—Insights from Theory and Practice*. Verlag Berlin Heidelberg: Springer: 29–45.

Schoff, James L. and Asei Ito (2019) 'Competing with China on Technology and Innovation,' *Carnegie Endowment for International Peace*: https://carnegieendowment.org/2019/10/10/competing-with-china-on-technology-and-innovation-pub-80010.

Schelling, Thomas C. (1980) *The Strategy of Conflict*. Cambridge, Massachusetts and London: Harvard University Press.

Schelling, Thomas C. (1960) *The Strategy of Conflict*. Oxford: Oxford University Press.

Schelling, Thomas C. (1960) 'Meteors, Mischief, and War,' *Bulletin of the Atomic Scientists*, 16 (7): 292–300.

Schelling, Thomas C. and Morton H. Halperin (1961) *Strategy and Arms Control*. New York, NY: Twentieth Century Fund.

Scobell, Andrew and Andrew J. Nathan (2012) 'China's Overstretched Military,' *Washington Quarterly*, 35 (4): 135–148.

Short, Nicola (1999) 'The Role of NGOs in the Ottawa Process to Ban Landmines,' *International Negotiation*, 4 (3): 483–502.

Seligman, Lara and Robbie Gramer (2019) 'Trump asks Tokyo to Quadruple Payments for U.S. Troops in Japan,' *Foreign Policy*: https://foreignpolicy.com/2019/11/15/trump-asks-tokyo-quadruple-payments-us-troops-japan/.

Smith, Steve (1984) 'US-Soviet Strategic Nuclear Arms Control: From SALT to START to Stop,' *Arms Control*, 5 (3): 50–74.

Sokov, Nikolai (2003) 'The Russian Nuclear Arms Control Agenda after SORT,' *Arms Control Today*, 33 (3): 7–11.

Smura, Tomasz (2016) 'Russian Anti-Access Area Denial (A2AD) Capabilities-Implications for NATO,' *Pulaski Policy*, 1–7. https://pulaski.pl/en/russian-anti-access-area-denial-a2ad-capabilities-implications-for-nato/

Speier, Richard H. George Nacouzi, Car-rie Lee and Richard M. Moore (2017) *Hypersonic Missile Nonproliferation: Hindering the Spread of a New Class of Weapons*. Santa Monica, CA: RAND Corporation.

Stone, Richard (2020) 'National Pride is at Stake. Russian, China and United States Race to Build Hypersonic Weapons,' *American Association for the Advancement of Science* https://www.sciencemag.org/news/2020/01/national-pride-stake-russia-china-united-states-race-build-hypersonic-weapons.

Tellis, Ashley J. Alsion Szalwinski and Michael Wills (eds.) (2017) *Strategic Asia 2017-18: Power, Ideas and Military Strategy in the Asia-Pacific*. Washington, DC: National Bureau of Asian Research.

Tennenwald, Nina (2018) 'The Great Unraveling: The Future of the Nuclear Normative Order,' in Nina Tennenwald and James M. Acton with an introduction by Jane Vaynman (eds.), *Meeting the Challenges of New Nuclear Age: Emerging Risks and Declining Norms in the Age of Technological Innovation and Changing Nuclear Doctrines.* Cambridge: American Academy of Arts and Sciences: 6–31.

Tong, Zhao (March 2017) 'China's Strategic Environment and Doctrine,' in Robert Einhorn and W. P. S. Sidhu (eds.), *The Strategic: Linking Pakistan, India, China and the United States.* Washington, DC: Brookings Institution: 17–24.

Trachtenberg, Marc (1991) 'The Past and Future of Arms Control,' *Daedalus*, 120 (1): 203–216.

Trenin, Dmitri (March, 2019) 'Strategic Stability in the Changing World,' *Carnegie Moscow Centre*, 1–11. https://carnegieendowment.org/files/3-15_Trenin_StrategicStability.pdf

Troianovski, Anton (2018) 'Putin Claims Russia is Developing Nuclear Arms Capable of Avoiding Missile Defenses,' *The Washington Post.* https://www.washingtonpost.com/world/europe/putin-claims-russia-has-nuclear-arsenal-capable-of-avoiding-missile-defenses/2018/03/01/d2dcf522-1d3b-11e8-b2d9-08e748f892c0_story.html

Veer, Ben Ter (1988) 'The Struggle against the Deployment of Cruise Missiles: The Learning Process of the Dutch Peace Movement,' *Bulletin of Peace Proposals*, 19 (02): 213–222.

Walker, William (2000) 'Nuclear Order and Disorder,' *International Affairs*, 76 (4): 703–724.

Whall, Helena and Allison Pytlak, (November, 2014) 'The Role of Civil Society in the International Negotiations on the Arms Trade Treaty,' *Global Policy*, 5 (4): 453–468.

Williams, Heather (2019) 'Asymmetric Arms Control and Strategic Stability: Scenarios for Limiting Hypersonic Glide Vehicles,' *Journal of Strategic Studies*, 42 (6): 789–813.

Williams, Heather (2018) 'A Nuclear Babel: Narratives around the Treaty on the Prohibition of Nuclear Weapons,' *The Nonproliferation Review*, 25 (1–2): 51–63.

Wittner, Lawrence S. (2003) 'The Forgotten Years of the World Nuclear Disarmament Movement, 1975-78,' *Journal of Peace Research*, 40 (4): 435–456.

Wohlstetter, Albert James (1958) 'The Delicate Balance of Terror,' *Foreign Affairs*, 37 (2): 211–234.

Ziegler, Charles E. (2014) 'Russian–American Relations: From Tsarism to Putin,' *International Politics*, 51 (6): 671–692.

Zeigler, Charles E. (2018) 'International Dimensions of Electoral Processes: Russia, the USA, and the 2016 Elections,' *International Politics*, 55 (5): 557–574.

Index

For Product Safety Concerns and Information please contact our EU
representative GPSR@taylorandfrancis.com
Taylor & Francis Verlag GmbH, Kaufingerstraße 24, 80331 München, Germany